All Gone

Also by Alex Witchel

Girls Only

Me Times Three

The Spare Wife

RIVERHEAD BOOKS
a member of Penguin Group (USA) Inc.
New York
2012

All Gone

A Memoir

of My

Mother's

Dementia.

With Refreshments

· · · · · ● · · · ·

Alex
Witchel

RIVERHEAD BOOKS
Published by the Penguin Group
Penguin Group (USA) Inc., 375 Hudson Street, New York, New York 10014, USA • Penguin Group
(Canada), 90 Eglinton Avenue East, Suite 700, Toronto, Ontario M4P 2Y3, Canada (a division of Pearson
Penguin Canada Inc.) • Penguin Books Ltd, 80 Strand, London WC2R 0RL, England • Penguin
Ireland, 25 St Stephen's Green, Dublin 2, Ireland (a division of Penguin Books Ltd) • Penguin Group
(Australia), 250 Camberwell Road, Camberwell, Victoria 3124, Australia (a division of Pearson Australia
Group Pty Ltd) • Penguin Books India Pvt Ltd, 11 Community Centre, Panchsheel Park, New Delhi–
110 017, India • Penguin Group (NZ), 67 Apollo Drive, Rosedale, North Shore 0632, New Zealand
(a division of Pearson New Zealand Ltd) • Penguin Books (South Africa) (Pty) Ltd,
24 Sturdee Avenue, Rosebank, Johannesburg 2196, South Africa

Penguin Books Ltd, Registered Offices: 80 Strand, London WC2R 0RL, England

ISBN 978-1-59448-791-0

Printed in the United States of America
10 9 8 7 6 5 4 3 2 1

BOOK DESIGN BY SUSAN WALSH

The recipes contained in this book are to be followed exactly as written. The publisher is
not responsible for your specific health or allergy needs that may require medical supervision.
The publisher is not responsible for any adverse reactions to the recipes contained in this book.

Penguin is committed to publishing works of quality and integrity.
In that spirit, we are proud to offer this book to our readers;
however, the story, the experiences, and the words
are the author's alone.

To Frank, Nat, and Simon,

with gratitude and love

All Gone

One

T he meat loaf fooled me.

I should have known it would. That's what a meat loaf is meant to do: make you believe the world is so forgiving a place that even an array of bits and pieces, all smashed up, can still find meaning as an eloquent whole. The duplicity is integral to the dish, if you make it well. And mine was perfect. Maybe not to you, or to someone else with opinions, someone named, say, Hungrydog4, who would tell you he's eaten plenty of meat loaf in his day and a meat loaf without ground pork is not a meat loaf at all. But when I made my mother's meat loaf for the first time, I could practically hear the garage door open, the car pull in. Mommy was home.

I used to watch her make the meat loaf. This was not a romantic endeavor. She never gloried in the squish of it—the part when you run your fingers through the cool ground meat just for fun. She is not a girl who has ever played with her food. Making dinner for her husband and four children was an obligation. It was also the center of the day, its organizing principle. We would leave the house each morning knowing what was for dinner because she would start it before she left to teach.

For meat loaf, she'd defrost a block of chopped meat wrapped in brown paper inside a plastic bag. Not in the refrigerator, where we now know it is safer, but on the counter, where the job would get done. By the time she returned at the end of the day, blood pooled around the seams of the paper, and you could push the bag with your finger and leave a dent. When she unwrapped it, some of the meat was brown, not red. This did not concern her.

Also in the morning, before leaving the house, she would check that she had two eggs, glancing inside the refrigerator door at the scooped-out top shelf where the eggs sat, naked and available, without benefit of an expiration date stamped on the end of a carton. This did not concern her, either.

Back home, in the late afternoon, she would cook while I set the table. She grated the onions into a bowl, swiping at a tear with her forearm. She beat the eggs before mixing them into the meat along with tomato soup. The best part was the cornflakes. She would crush a few handfuls before adding them. They gave the meat loaf something of a golden aura, to my eye at least. She turned the contents of the bowl into a pan—the black pan with white speckles—and shaped it into an oval. There was no rack or tray on the bottom to drain the fat. Fat was what made it taste good.

Then she would empty a can of Le Sueur peas into a pot and set it on the stove. In another black speckled pan, she would toss some cubed potatoes in oil, sprinkle them with salt, pepper, and paprika, and set them above the meat loaf to bake. When I make them, I parboil them first, so they end up creamy on the inside and crispy on the outside. She would scoff at this innovation—extra time, extra pot. But I know she would approve of my throwing the onions into the Cuisinart, zapping them into the watery mush great chefs tell us to avoid. Because neither one of us likes to cry.

After the first time I made the meat loaf, I felt pretty invincible. Yes, it is a simple recipe, but even simple recipes can suffer in the wrong hands. I had the touch. With three pounds of chopped meat, I could erase years, play with time. The meat loaf was a magic charm.

Until it wasn't.

I picture Mom in her kitchen. It is a cheerful room, wallpapered in white crisscrossed with arbors of red roses. It is sometime in the 1970s. She is just home from work, wearing a black-and-white tweed skirt and a white turtleneck. Her hair is blond and teased, like Farrah Fawcett's. Her broad cheekbones and wide-set brown eyes balance her strong jaw. Her face is perfectly symmetrical, hard and soft at once. She is beautiful in a way I will never be, and this has never bothered me. I love looking at her.

After a long day of teaching, she can be short on patience. This is one of those days. She does not make conversation. She gets on with it. That is her forte, getting on with it. She stands near the stove while I fold yellow paper napkins in half diagonally and turn the knife blades toward the plates because she actually checks things like that. Her back is to me. She is absorbed in her tasks.

"Mom!" I call. "I need your help. I made the meat loaf and it was perfect. I made the potatoes and I added a step—they're actually better. I made the same peas because some things don't change and don't need to. I did everything right. Every damn thing you ever told me to do. My knives faced in. I came home on time. I married a good man. I have a good job. I didn't have children, but no one's perfect."

"So?" I see her profile, slightly annoyed that I'm distracting her in the middle of making dinner for six people. It really isn't the time to bother her with this. Maybe later, when she's scrubbing the pan and I'm making the lunches for the next day, slicing the meat loaf and fitting each slab inside a kaiser roll, spreading ketchup along the tops. Maybe after that, when she's showered and put on a clean flannel nightgown, sitting down in the den in front of the TV, lighting a cigarette. Once she's out of the kitchen, she's happier, calmer.

But I need her to stay in the kitchen now, in command mode. I need her to tell me what to do. She walks past me. "Dinner!" she yells, in that strangely muted way she has, moving her voice to the back of her throat, apologizing for yelling even as she does it. With a spatula, she scrapes the potatoes out of the pan and into a bowl. She strains the water from the peas. She turns the meat loaf onto a plate in an instant. I'm terrible at that. I worry it will break.

The food is on the table and the family is seated now. None of them hears me. Or if they do, none of them looks up.

"Wait," I implore her. "You have to answer my questions. So many awful things have happened and I'm not sure how to handle them. You have to tell me. Please."

She leans over the stove to make sure the low light under the peas is turned off. I can't see her face. "You have excellent judgment," I hear her say. "I know you will make the right decisions."

"But what if I don't? I need your help."

I look at the stove. She is gone.

The moments, awkward and fleeting, started casually enough, little tickles of annoyance more than alarm. In 2000, in the middle of a seder with my stepsons, Nat and Simon, Mom called Nat "Nate." He seemed surprised, hurt even. She didn't remember his name? I growled at her about it, sotto voce, while we fussed over a serving platter. When she remained silent, I figured she was embarrassed.

At my brother Emmett's wedding in 2004, she wore a lavender shirtwaist, its matching fabric belt consistently askew, revealing the elastic beneath. My mother has never been a stylish dresser (much to my sister Phoebe's chagrin), but she has always been a fastidious dresser. Making sure that belt had loops to hold it in place was the kind of thing she would do automatically.

One night, she and my father saw a movie with friends, one I had already seen. I asked her opinion of a plot point, and it became clear she hadn't followed the story. She changed the subject.

Like I said, little tickles. People misspeak—we actually had a relative named Nate. Errant belt loops on a wedding day might not be paramount to someone who doesn't care about clothes. Not recalling a movie plot? I can't remember the movie in question myself.

But during the course of the next year, she didn't seem quite right. She kept telling me she was tired, she who was famous for never taking naps. The family joke had always been that if she lay down in daylight, she'd need to be shot. Like a horse.

I bought a new dress, not fancy, what she and I would call a schmatta dress, to cook in, wear around the house. It was navy with three buttons beneath the collar, each of a distinctly different design. When she saw the buttons, she recoiled. "What's wrong with that dress?" she shouted. "Why don't the buttons match?"

"It's the design," I said. "They're not supposed to match." That didn't mollify her. She stayed rattled, and although she didn't say anything else, she continued to glare at both me and the dress.

I dismissed the incident at the time, but I have thought of it frequently since, her off-kilter reaction to something so small. I know now what I missed then. It was about order. The buttons weren't uniform. And in her state, that suddenly felt like chaos.

One day, Phoebe called me, distraught. A friend at work told her she'd logged on to a website where college students comment on their professors. Someone had posted a complaint about Mom. She was too old to teach. She had given the same lecture twice.

"Completely untrue!" I thundered. "You know it was just some kid who was failing, seeking revenge." Phoebe knew no such thing, but we agreed never to mention it. We made it our secret.

When Mom "decided" to retire a few months later, we knew it was not our secret at all.

By the following September, she was still tired, and I insisted we see a neurologist together. It turned out that she'd already seen one, Jesse Weinberger at Mount Sinai Hospital, the year before. He'd done those Doppler radar tests that determine whether or not your carotid arteries, a station of the cross of cardiovascular disease, are in working order. Once we were in his office, I learned that the results had been dicey enough to warrant retesting, but my mother never came back.

Was she actually sent a reminder card? I asked stiffly. Weinberger opened the file and showed me three dates on which three different cards had been sent. It didn't surprise me that she would ignore them; she never put much stock in doctors and avoided them whenever possible. That she wouldn't remember receiving the reminders, however, was unthinkable. Yet that's exactly what she said. She didn't remember.

Weinberger repeated the Doppler and discovered that one artery had closed completely; the other, 75 percent. This meant that my mother, the college professor, had 25 percent blood flow to her brain at this moment, which had been the situation for six months or more. That she had been teaching at all seemed astonishing.

I struggled to contain my panic, asking questions, taking notes. Keeping track. That had always been my job. Or at least I thought it was. When Weinberger asked her what medications she was taking, and which doctor had prescribed which pill for which illness, she hesitated. I leapt in authoritatively, starting to recite. Quite firmly, he asked me to stop; he was addressing my mother. She continued the list while I listened, feeling light-headed. She was naming doctors I had never heard of, medications I had no idea had been prescribed. Over the past couple of years, she had told me repeatedly that she was fine. Why hadn't she told me the truth?

Weinberger instructed her to collect all the medications she was taking and bring them in. At the next visit, she placed two bulging plastic bags on his desk. There were easily thirty bottles of pills, mostly antidepressants in differing doses. When he asked her why she was taking them, she squinted at some of the labels, as if the answers would be written there. She made jokes and smiled coyly. She didn't know.

I was equally baffled. When had this happened? Why hadn't I seen it more clearly? Most important, how fast could we fix it?

Not fast at all. Tests and procedures, small and large, loomed. Each test led to another appointment, to another procedure. We sat side by side in endless waiting rooms. My mother had trouble filling out the forms. She couldn't seem to make the pen move the way she wanted. On the first few visits, she recited her Social Security number by heart as I wrote it down. But when she started handing me her Medicare card, I realized she could no longer remember it. I filled out so many forms for her that when I saw a new doctor for myself the following year, I gave my birth date as 1931.

"Have you had any surgeries?" a technician asked her a few

weeks after the one she had to fix the carotid artery that could still be salvaged.

"No," she said.

"Yes," I said.

"You make a good team," he said.

As my mother began the torturous process of disappearing in plain sight, I retreated to my kitchen, trying to reclaim her at the stove. Is there any contract tighter than a family recipe? Just do as I say and *poof!* Here I am, good as new. Or something like that. Picking up a pot was not the instant panacea for illness and isolation and utter despair that I wanted it to be. But it helped. When I turned to the food, I felt grounded in my mother's rules, and they worked every time.

I could overcook or undercook the meat loaf and it still tasted the same. I could use ground turkey instead of beef and veal and it tasted remarkable—for turkey meat loaf. I could eat it hot and eat it cold, and I ended up doing both because Nat and Simon and my husband, Frank, like meat loaf fine, but they don't love it. Peg Bracken summed it up perfectly in *The I Hate to Cook Book*. Men prefer steaks and chops to casseroles and meat loaf, she wrote, because they "like a tune they can whistle." But it was those inexact elements, murky and mystical, that drew me to my mother's meat loaf again and again. It was my remnant of home and I conjured it, reaching back, always back. Each time I made it, it was absolutely perfect. And each time I made it, I felt more and more afraid.

Meat Loaf

· ·

1 ½ pounds ground chuck
1 ½ pounds ground veal
1 large or 2 medium onions
2 eggs, beaten
1 can tomato soup (not cream of tomato)
4 handfuls (or more) cornflakes
Salt and pepper

Preheat oven to 350°F.

Place meat in a large mixing bowl. Grate onion and add to meat.
Mix in the eggs, then the soup. Crush the cornflakes in your
hands and add to the bowl. Add salt and pepper and mix
thoroughly—mixture should be firm enough to hold together
when molded. (If the mixture is too loose, add more cornflakes.)

Shape the meat into a loaf in a baking pan just large enough to
hold it. Bake for 1 hour.

Serves 4, with leftovers for sandwiches

Paprika Potatoes

· ·

Adapted from A Passion for Potatoes: 200 Recipes for Appetizers, Entrees, Side Dishes, Even Desserts *by Lydie Marshall (Harper Perennial).*

> 2 pounds Yukon Gold potatoes
> 1/3 cup canola oil
> Paprika
> Salt and pepper

Preheat oven to 350°F.

Cut the potatoes into 1 ½-inch cubes. In a large saucepan, cover the potatoes with cold salted water and bring to a boil. Turn off the heat and drain the potatoes.

Place a roasting pan or large cast-iron skillet over high heat on top of the stove and add the oil. When the oil is hot, add the potatoes and carefully toss them to coat. Sprinkle liberally with paprika, salt, and pepper.

Place the pan in the oven (if baking with the meat loaf, place on the rack above) and roast for 45 minutes to an hour, turning the potatoes occasionally, until they are golden brown on all sides. Serve immediately.

Serves 4

Two

··●·····

My first memory of my mother is of her standing in front of the open refrigerator, head thrown back, laughing. She is huge—tall and rounded under a great swath of flannel; she must have been pregnant with my brother Greg. She is holding a glass bottle of milk—this was when we lived in our house on Terhune Avenue in Passaic, New Jersey, in the days when the butter-and-egg man left his delivery at the side door.

Why was he called that, I wanted to know, when all he brought us was milk, and Mom bought her butter and eggs at the supermarket? Because in the old days, Mom said, before there were supermarkets, he would bring butter and eggs to your home. Delivering milk was an innovation that let him compete with the milkman. So even though he brought milk, he was still not the milkman. In our house, it was always the old days.

That I asked the question, though, was what made her happy. Getting to the bottom of things was a worthy pursuit. Every day when she and I would come home from school, she would sit me down at the kitchen table. "Tell me everything that happened today," she'd say. That meant recounting every last moment, starting with the school bus that morning. If she asked questions, I had to have answers. She praised me for my recall, for noticing tiny details.

She always liked telling her own story about bringing me home from the hospital as a newborn. "Your father and I were sitting at the breakfast table and I looked over at your carriage"— she drew herself up, surprised—"and there you were, lifting your head up, trying to see what was going on. Three days old and you didn't want to miss a thing. So alert!"

"Alert," "bright," "aware"—these were the words that made my mother happiest. "Quick on the uptake" was another pet phrase. Anything that proved you were on top of your game. Not that you were "doing your best"—a slick excuse in her book— but that your best got results. On the first day of school, Mom would kiss each of us, hold our heads in her hands while looking deep into our eyes, and say, "May you be brilliant."

The first rule of brilliance, certainly, was knowing that Mom was always right. She lived her life as an act of will, and her will was formidable. My father posed as the ultimate authority, as most fathers did once upon a time. But a few well-placed whacks aside, Mom ran the show. "Did you wash your hands?" she would ask us routinely. We stopped saying yes routinely when she made us hold them out, palms up, in order to gauge the degree of gray, then flip them, to spy the telltale grime beneath the nails. She peered deep inside our ears, wielding Q-tips. When we protested, she told us that if she didn't clean them out, peas and carrots would grow there. She washed our hair in the bath, which we hated, tipping our heads back and back to rinse out the suds with cupfuls of water. When we complained, she said that if our hair got too dirty, it would get up and walk off our heads. Every day, she would stand me in front of her and run her thumbs over my eyebrows, training them to go in the right direction, she claimed. No detail was too small for her inventory. Even in my incipiently bratty teenage years, when she signed off on a letter she sent me at sleepaway camp as "The One Who Always Knows Best," I did not scoff at her use of rhetoric. I accepted the self-designated title as the statement of fact I knew it to be.

She was meticulous in the way she dressed, and in the way she dressed us. I remember her lifting me off her in the front seat of the car on a summer day, catching my swinging feet in one hand, and setting me back down, none too gently, beside her. She was wearing a white pleated skirt, and I must have been climbing on her in that unconscious way kids do, as if their parents are well-padded jungle gyms built specifically for their use. Somehow I hadn't considered that the soles of my shoes were a potential danger to the skirt. I assumed Mom would remain perfectly Mom, in spite of my transgressions.

The rigor of her work schedule shaped our days. Mornings were a blur of fights about oatmeal, Wheatena, or Cream of Wheat, which she served salted, a cold lump of butter melting into a pool of yellow slime at the center of the bowl. I refused to eat any of them. Finally, both of us would have to leave for school. I would leave tearstained but triumphant. It was one of the few things she couldn't break me on.

Mom was not home most days when our school ended, but she found a way to turn every minute of our downtime into activities. I had Hebrew school and Brownies, ballet and piano lessons, and Monday afternoons at the public library. Evenings were an early dinner for me, Greg, and Mom, followed by baths that were simultaneously spelling bees. There I wormed my way back into her heart after the hot cereal standoffs of the morning. I was good.

Her greatest, and vainest, hope was to dump us in bed by seven, so she could unfurl her papers—exams to grade or her doctoral thesis in progress—across the expanse of the dining room table. We had other ideas. The first was awaiting the arrival of my father, who came home to a plate of food that looked infinitely more wonderful than ours ever did. Mom saved him the biggest, most burnished piece of meat, the fluffiest pile of mashed potatoes. I eyed that plate like I hadn't eaten in weeks, begging for tastes, which he gladly gave me. Often he brought home some exotic piece of fruit for dessert—mango, papaya, one time even a coconut that required a hammer to crack it open. She may have resented his sabotaging our bedtime, but in our house nothing but God was holier than education, and even tropical fruit was education of a sort. We made it to bed soon thereafter, and Mom's papers unfurled only slightly behind schedule. She managed never to be more than momentarily derailed in the endless budgeting of her time or the equally endless minding of our manners.

She was adamant on good posture and our saying "yes" in answer to a question, never "yeah." "Please," "Thank you," and "Excuse me" were mandatory. When I see children now running rampant through restaurants or whining at their mother as she speaks to another adult—or, God forbid, pulling at her sleeve—I think of my mother and fear for their lives.

Outbursts or interruptions from her own children evoked The Look: tight mouth, slightly narrowed eyes telegraphing an absence of mirth tinged with the long dark shadow of eternal damnation. To be on the receiving end of The Look was worse than an actual punishment; hanging in the balance between Mom's good graces and bad was an excruciating purgatory where the dread of the potential fall was its own particular pain. She had no hesitation about spanking us, yanking us, or yelling at us if we misbehaved. And if someone else's children misbehaved, she felt free to spank, yank, or yell at them, too. She just missed the current fashion of not disciplining other people's children, and I have no doubt she would have scorned it. In her book, bad behavior was bad behavior, and the only way to eradicate it was to punish it, especially if others were too soft—or lazy—to do the job themselves.

She turned her own downtime into activities, too. At the house on Terhune Avenue, she kept a lush flower garden that ran the entire length of the backyard. She spent hours out there on her knees, ministering to a rosebush or a row of hyacinths, her rough gloves encased in dirt, using her forearm to scratch her nose, the same way she would in the kitchen when her hands were full of onions. In the colder months, she volunteered, reading books for the blind. When she was seven months pregnant with Emmett, she went up and down the block to every house in the neighborhood with a political petition. When she sat in front of the TV, she hooked rugs. And in her spare time—when was that, exactly?— she took a sculpture class.

She could be as hard on us as she was on herself, but most of the time she treated us more kindly and gently. She would spend hours coloring with me, and even when my periwinkle Crayola went outside the lines, she praised my efforts effusively. She bought me *Meet the Beatles!* letting me play it over and over again, and took me to see the movie version of *The Odd Couple* at night, like a grown-up. She taught me how to play checkers and chess and never to cheat at Monopoly. When she took me with her on her errands, we often ended up side by side at the counter of a candy store in Passaic, watching our chocolate malted drop, as if in slow motion, from the metal canister into our waiting glasses.

On Halloween, she could make me look like a cat with only an eye pencil, and was so delighted by her handiwork that she called me Pussycat forever after. When she put makeup on me, just for fun, she could see into the future, how pretty I would be when I grew up. She dabbed my wrists with Joy, as she did her own, and when she went out at night she also put some behind her knees. "Someone lovely just walked by," she'd say, laughing at how silly that was. But she said it every time, which was part of the fun. She was fierce in her protection of us, and I was equally fierce in my devotion to her.

She was smarter than Donna Reed, even nicer than June Cleaver, and if not quite as hilarious as Lucille Ball, no less resourceful. One time she needed a new outfit—maybe for a presentation or a class. We sat around, just us girls, scheming about how she would persuade Dad to pay for it. I had recently compiled a list of odd jobs I could charge for, and to it I'd added *Problem Solving, 1 cent*. She tried me out, but in the end it was her plan that prevailed. When Dad got home, she said, she would put on some music to relax him, then sit and talk to him in the living room. It sounded like a movie. I was dying to see it.

That night, I slipped out of bed and crouched midway down the stairs leading to the living room. There was music. There was conversation. I couldn't hear much of it, but it sounded boring. No mention of clothes. I went to bed. The next morning, I braced myself for defeat. "All set," she said, smiling. I was awestruck. She could get exactly what she wanted by talking about something else? She was magical.

I wanted to be magical, too. In the backyard one day I told her I was going to become a doctor and needed to examine her. She seemed quite interested in this news. I asked her to raise her arm, which she did, and I scrutinized the stubble in her armpit, murmuring some diagnosis. She burst out laughing. I was crushed. This was not funny! She was working so hard to become a doctor, I wanted to be a doctor, too! Frustrated, I stopped scrutinizing her armpit and started punching it. I can still see the lawn passing beneath my squalling face as she hauled me back to the house and dumped me in solitary.

The one thing she remained resolutely humorless about was honesty. She loved it when the things I told her about my day made her laugh—that is, if they were true. To be clear, what she loved was accurate reporting. She did not love storytelling. Making things up was a sucker's way out.

I learned that lesson hard and early on the unfortunate day I told my first-grade class that sheep lived in our basement. That was not my finest hour, but I was suffering envy in the extreme. My teacher, Mrs. Israel, had asked each of us to describe our pets. One after the other, kids talked about their dogs and cats and hamsters and turtles—which were legal then, I know, because we had two of them until Mom moved the couch to vacuum and squashed one into the wall-to-wall carpeting.

The other kids told story after story featuring frisky puppies chasing balls or backlit aquariums adorned with zebra-striped fish and miniature castles moored in the sand. Finally, there was Stacy Silverstein, who had a Saint Bernard. She said he was so big she could climb onto his back and ride him like a horse. Well, I knew I'd never succeed in persuading my parents to get a Saint Bernard, but in the unlikely event I did, I would never be allowed to ride him like a horse. We had no dogs of any kind, and no cats, either, because Dad was allergic to them—or he claimed to be. I suspect he was allergic to the cost of their upkeep.

Our sole pet, after the demise of the turtles (the second one must have died of loneliness, or fear of the vacuum cleaner), was a yellow parakeet named Specksie. This was after Mom's childhood dog, who was black and white and had specks around his face that looked like freckles. It was not an imaginative name for a dog, but at least it was a logical one. Specksie the bird had no specks. No matter where I stood, she made no eye contact. The only thing she ever did that was remotely interactive was to escape her cage when it was being cleaned and fly to the top of the drapes in the living room. This sent both my parents into waves of hysteria, because the last thing the living room was meant for was living. It was mostly for show, and the show did not feature avian excrement.

So Specksie was a bust on the companion front, though I did think of her years later while interviewing a woman for a magazine piece. She told me that if you took the name of your first pet and paired it with the name of the first street you lived on, that would be your stripper name. Which meant that if I had ever become a stripper, my name would be Specksie Terhune.

But in first grade, I had no idea about strippers. All I cared about was competing in the sweepstakes for the greatest pet of our times. I raised my hand and announced that in our basement lived a family of sheep. There was a mother sheep and a father sheep and four baby sheep. I described them in great detail—their curly white hair and black hooves and bulging eyes that looked like grapes. Mrs. Israel's own eyes bulged as she asked me question after question. I answered them all.

And then the bell rang and I forgot about it. I went home for lunch, where Mom was actually in residence that day, serving peanut butter and jelly on Wonder Bread and pouring milk, just like Donna Reed without the apron. I always wished she would cut the crusts off the Wonder Bread, like some other mothers did, which made the sandwiches seem like more fun, but she found that wasteful. So while I chewed the crusts dutifully, the phone rang and she left the table for what turned into an awfully long time. I heard her voice in the other room shift from bright and cheery to low and serious, with lots of drawn-out *hmmmm*s. Then she was back. In those days, she wore her hair in a black Jackie bubble and sported glittery blue cat-eye glasses that looked pretty with her red lipstick. But at that moment, her red lipstick was not smiling and the glasses took on a sinister glint. I stopped chewing.

That was Mrs. Israel on the line, Mom said. She had been so taken by my account of the sheep in the basement that she wanted to arrange a field trip for the class to visit them. What did they eat? she'd wanted to know. How often? Did they go into the yard for exercise?

In retrospect, I have to wonder whether Mrs. Israel was one gullible broad, or saw me for the bold-faced liar I was and called Mom to bust me. I never did find out. After an endless session of sheep interrogation, Mom delivered her verdict: overactive imagination. Well, okay, maybe I did have one. What was wrong with that? What was wrong, she countered, was that it was just another way of saying I was a liar. And how many times had she told me that lying was a sin, equaled perhaps by no other?

I had quite a few days to ponder that question, since whenever she was mad at me Mom gave me the silent treatment. I chose the basement as the appropriate site to lick my psychic wounds. This was a finished basement, as it was called, with a bar built into one wall. The bar remained distressingly bare for the five years we lived in that house; in their early married years, my parents prided themselves on their abstemiousness when it came to hard liquor in the home.

Anyway, my point about the basement was the floor. It was covered in some sort of green rubber and branded in the middle with a big black swirling P, enclosed in a circle. That was for *Pashman*, which was the name of the family from whom my parents had bought the house. Why hadn't they changed it to a W when we moved in? I had asked. Too expensive was the answer. The eternal answer.

Well, my six-year-old self reasoned, down there in the cold green Siberia of the former Pashman residence, was it not a *lie* that we lived in a house identified with the wrong letter? If it said P, didn't that mean it was still the Pashman house, and they could move back any time they liked? What about that? Maybe those sheep belonged to the Pashmans.

I don't remember making much progress with that argument. Then, when my report card came, I got a "Needs Improvement" in "Following Directions," which, on top of my overactive imagination, just about did Mom in. So she established some structure. That was when she instituted the Monday trips to the library, where I would take out exactly six books. Until I could read alone, Mom read them to me, one a day for a week with one day off for good behavior. When I could read on my own, I had to finish all the books I had chosen, or present a full-blown case for an exemption, which might or might not be granted.

Then, errands. Mom ran lots of errands and she took me with her. It was her job to shop for the family and make sure everything in the house worked, and she made sure I understood that, too. First we would go to the butcher. The butcher shop was one of those battlefields that Mom was forever fighting on. You would think she could simply say, "I want four rib-eye steaks," and watch the butcher lift them from the glass case. But no. Nothing in the front of the shop was good enough. That was for the goyim, those sad fools who didn't know the difference between good meat and great. (Why non-Jews would be shopping in a kosher butcher shop that was more expensive than a non-kosher butcher shop and was missing so many delicious meats and appealing cuts was never explained.) The great meat was always in the back, tucked out of sight. Fresh. Special. If you were in the know, you requested to have it cut in front of you.

Mom did not manufacture this myth herself. Nana, my father's mother and the greatest cook in the family, thought this, too, and so did the other women at the synagogue. All these years later I can only surmise that the poor butcher kept most of his inventory in the back so that when these lunatics approached he could give them the exact same thing everyone else got, except that he walked three extra steps for it, which made them happy. What made me happy was that every time I came in, he put a fat bologna in the slicer and handed over a floppy piece, wide and pink and fragrant with garlic. That slice of bologna was one of the most perfect foods I would ever eat, and I knew that at the age of six as immutably as I knew my own name.

On Thanksgiving, we picked up our specially ordered turkey—stowed in the back with all the rest of them—then went on to the florist for the centerpiece. Mom oohed and aahed over every last arrangement as I stared at the tightly curled long-stem roses behind the closed glass doors, because I didn't care about plants and pots and dirt like she did. At last she would take her cornucopia, a dark brown wicker horn filled with autumn leaves and rust-colored chrysanthemums and yellow and white carnations, and hold it stiffly in front of her, while the owner rushed to open the door. When I grew older and discovered from posh people who Know About Flowers that carnations are cheap and repellent, I was chagrined. They always smelled clean and garden-fresh and looked like the best party you could ever look forward to. I loved them.

If it was an ordinary day of errands, we'd skip the florist and stop at the dry cleaner. The shop was stifling, and I hated the whirring of the mechanized rack and the hot chemical breath of the plastic-wrapped clothes as they whipped around. Once, when we got back into the car, Mom discovered that the man behind the counter had given her four dollars change from the ten she gave him to pay for eight dollars' worth of cleaning.

"You made two dollars!" I crowed.

"No, I did not." The iron door of disapproval slammed down. "Listen to me," Mom said. "That man is in business to support his family. He has children just like you to feed and clothe. He made a mistake giving me too much change, and if I take it, that money comes out of his family's expenses. We are going back."

Okay, okay. I could not, would not, tell a lie.

Inside the house, Mom's biggest responsibility was cooking. With the exception of the all-too-infrequent pot of My-T-Fine chocolate pudding, which she allowed me and Greg to stir, she and I never cooked together because she never considered cooking fun. It was her obligation to feed four, then (as Phoebe and Emmett came along), five and six people, three times a day. By Sunday brunch, except on the special occasions when there were bagels and lox, you could actually taste the hostility she imparted to a tomato omelet: the pale, cottony tomato shedding clumps of watery seeds into the rubbery mat of eggs expressed exactly what she thought about every single one of us at that moment when she would rather have stayed in bed.

Though she did teach me how to bake cookies and tell when a cake was done, she generally encouraged me to learn by osmosis, watching her. Occasionally I had a brainstorm on her behalf, like spiking the pot of Le Sueur peas with a few shots of A.1. sauce; though come to think of it, she never asked me to repeat that one. Mostly, she cooked and I watched.

Though Mom could be fearless when cooking from scratch— the homemade crepes for her cheese blintzes were a thing of beauty to behold—she usually favored shortcuts. Like most women of her generation, she was obsessed with convenience foods—frozen or canned vegetables, bottled salad dressing, Lawry's Seasoned Salt, and Accent, the now reviled MSG. The bomb-shelter mentality of the late 1950s and early 1960s pervaded our house; Del Monte was her farmer's market. Everything was in season, and syrup, all the time.

The worst food product (or imitation food product) Mom insisted on using was Bac-Os, which were made with soybeans and were the color of dried blood. She mixed them into scrambled eggs because they were supposed to taste like bacon. Their meatless, acrid saltiness tasted nothing like bacon. Just hearing her shake them from the jar into a bowl of beaten raw eggs was an invitation for Sunday night blues to begin at noon.

Along with her fondness for synthetic food products, Mom loved modern gadgets, like her electric can opener, a contraption I never understood. Using it took the same amount of time as the manual one did. Also in this category was the electric carving knife, operated by Dad, which seemed most effective as a shredder. But these are people who slept with electric blankets, so at least they were consistent.

Mom dealt with the drudgery of her kitchen chores by plotting two great escapes each week: dinner out on Fridays and Sundays. Early on, she and Dad fell into the pattern of claiming alone time on Friday nights; he would go to his health club after work, or to see a foreign movie that didn't interest her. She would take Greg and me out to dinner—at least until Phoebe and Emmett came along, by which time she was just as glad to collapse in front of *Dallas*.

But back then she drove a convertible, silver with red leather seats. She'd wrap a scarf around her hair and put the top down, signaling the start to a great adventure. Tonight it might be Pompeii Pizza, where Greg and I would each get a slice, a Coke, and a quarter for the jukebox. Or Giuliano's, where we two kids would eat pizza but she would pull out the stops for sausage and peppers with spaghetti on the side. The highlight of Giuliano's was the wishing well at the entrance, its bubbling water lit pink, piles of pennies twinkling at its depths. Then there was Ding Ho Palace, where she and Greg would start with spare ribs and I ate an egg roll before we moved on to her favorite, lobster Cantonese. Wherever our evenings started, they usually ended at Dairy Queen in a haze of bliss.

Sunday dinners always included Dad and ranged from deli to fancy French or Italian, the latter usually reserved for birthdays or other special occasions. Whatever the restaurant, we were not allowed to order from the children's menu, a point on which Dad was even more strict than Mom. Dining out was an opportunity for education, and he didn't want it wasted on a hamburger. Mom would always begin with a cocktail—Dewar's on the rocks with a splash of soda and a twist of lemon—and always end with dessert—chocolate cake, chocolate mousse, or banana splits with hot fudge.

Wherever she ate, in fact, Mom's daily reward was something sweet. Sugar was the chink in her armor. She kept an entire kitchen drawer stocked with a rotating selection of Oreos, Vienna Fingers, and Mallomars, and every Friday she bought her "downfall" from the Scarsdale Pastry Center: a loaf of marble cake coated in dark chocolate. There was never an evening school event that didn't end at Baskin-Robbins, and never a breakfast in a diner without waffles crowned with butter and syrup or, even better, whipped cream. When the concept of junk food was introduced in the 1970s, it made almost no impression on her. She stocked the kitchen drawer the same as always, though she was forced to replace Oreos with Hydrox when Oreos stopped being kosher for a while. She did start to bake a few things herself—like mandelbrot from a Manischewitz mix that had all the same additives the packaged cookies had.

Diets were more theoretical than actual in our house, the continual talk about them a low-grade lament, background music to both snacking and feasting. Mom tried Weight Watchers when she was pregnant with Emmett. It kept her weight gain reasonable, but once he was born, her efforts to stick with it were spotty. Once I became a teenager, I joined in. For me, the Scarsdale Diet was the worst; that water-packed canned tuna with lemon and vinegar lunch on Mondays was so upsetting. Lemon *and* vinegar? Was that really necessary?

Trying out for cheerleading in high school, I went to a practice at another girl's house. When we took a break, I reached for one of the cookies her mom had left on the kitchen table. Two of the girls physically recoiled, so repelled were they by my vulgar appetite. One of them had been on the cover of *Seventeen* magazine, which made her the gold standard for all things beauty-related, so of course I was instantly disgraced. I was also surprised. I thought skinny girls were born skinny and stayed that way, eating anything they wanted. Mom always talked about having a fat gene, and I knew that having one meant that diets worked only so much; there was nothing really to be done. Nor was there anything to be done about my lack of coordination. I did not become a cheerleader.

I eventually took up jogging, as was the fashion then. Surprisingly, Mom joined in for about a year, mustering her famous will, losing weight and looking fabulous. She cut down on smoking so she wouldn't gasp her way around the track at the high school where we ran. But soon enough, her innate orneriness kicked in. The elemental idiocy of running in circles rankled her. The pack mentality ended up irritating her, as it usually did. She retired her sneakers, lit a More cigarette—the longest ones on the market—and settled into her black leather recliner with a vodka and grapefruit juice in an icy wineglass. What do the doctors know anyway? she would snort. After all, when her grandmother, my greatgrandma Tessie, turned eighty, hadn't she famously polished off six bagels with cream cheese and lox at her birthday party, not to die until eighty-eight, after breaking a hip?

That was Mom's role model, certainly. When I was younger and I used to cry, afraid of death in general but of Mom's in particular, she would just laugh. "I don't have time to die," she'd proclaim. And she never did seem to get sick. During the sixty years she smoked half a pack a day, I remember her having a cold or sore throat only a handful of times, and the flu, never. She annually postponed her annual checkups. In the mid-1980s, when her doctor told her she was morbidly obese, she shrugged. Ran in the family. Sure, she had chronic bellyaches—"aggravation, that's why"—so she kept Maalox in every bag she owned, briefcase or peau de soie. If she didn't feel well, her fallback position was to take a hot shower and two aspirin. She'd revive, like a plant. The woman was unstoppable.

Or at least I thought she was. Until that moment in Weinberger's office when she placed the bags of pills on the desk. Before that day she never let me accompany her to a doctor. She hadn't wanted Dad to go with her, either. Why should she? Was she a child? There wasn't the slightest thing wrong with her.

Really? Then why was she so tired?

Getting older.

I believed her.

When I finally realized she needed real help, I centralized her care at Mount Sinai, where I could keep track of who was doing what and why.

A CT scan ordered by Weinberger showed she had suffered ministrokes, transient ischemic attacks. The scar tissue the strokes left in Mom's brain was anything but mini; because of its location, it was not only impairing her memory but trapping her in a state of exacerbated depression. Additionally, her circulation was poor enough that she required aortobifemoral bypass surgery. This referred to the aorta located in the abdomen (who knew?) that was blocked, so blood was not flowing to her lower extremities. She needed prosthetic veins transplanted in her abdomen and down through her legs to move the blood or she risked amputation.

Clearly, we needed to act quickly. For the mood and memory problems, Weinberger referred us to Martin Goldstein, a doctor new to Mount Sinai. He was both a psychiatrist and a neurologist, reputedly brainy and cutting-edge. He would part the Red Sea, and we would walk through it.

When we sat down in Goldstein's office for the first time, I watched Mom size him up. He was young, good-looking, and shy, short on eye contact and long on medical jargon. As he explicated the CT scan on a computer screen before us, he looked up for a split second. "Are you married?" Mom asked. I shot her my version of The Look, incredulous and warning. She widened her eyes innocently in return.

Goldstein blushed. "No, I'm not," he said courteously, smiling just a bit. From then on he addressed her directly. Soon, she started answering. As a lifelong reader of *Scientific American*, my mother appreciated a good brain image herself. When we left, he called her Dr. Witchel. Her face changed, and for a moment, it seemed she might cry. I could see her remember she actually was Dr. Witchel.

I so wanted her to be. And with a purse full of prescriptions—the right prescriptions at the right dosage—maybe she would be again. We left the office and I walked her to the corner, where she caught a cab to Grand Central. I went home. An hour or so later, the phone rang.

"Alex? It's Dad. I just got a phone call from the doorman at the apartment building next to the doctor's office. He found your mother's wallet on the sidewalk."

"He did? I was with her in front of that building and had no idea that happened. Where is she now? How is she going to get home?"

"Beats me. I haven't heard from her."

He did soon after. He drove in and picked her up, then together they retrieved her wallet.

It turned out that when she got to Grand Central and realized the wallet was gone, she explained this to her cabdriver and promised to send him a check, taking his name and address. The next day Mom put cash in an envelope and mailed it. "He was such a nice man," she told me. "I'm sure he thought he'd never see a dime."

"I thought you were sending him a check," I said.

She hesitated. "I don't want to identify myself," she said curtly.

"By the way," I asked, "how did you manage to call Dad?" Neither of my parents used a cell phone.

Her voice was small. "The driver," she said. "He gave me a quarter."

In 1997, still firm in the belief that my mother could be found on the other end of the phone for all eternity, I had asked her, as a birthday present to me, to write down twenty of her recipes. We're talking basic 1950s housewife food, kosher division—roast chicken, spaghetti and meat sauce, brisket. With a few exceptions, I had never gotten much past the meat loaf. My limited success had made me cocky: I was her and she was me, and if and when I decided to try out other of her dishes, I'd have the same results she did.

I had yet to attempt her chicken soup, the three-day affair she made for Rosh Hashanah and Passover, echt Jewish Mommy food. Simon first tasted it when he was six, and we all laughed, watching him scrape at the flowers imprinted on the bottom of the bowl to get the last drop.

Nor had I made the chicken and prunes, another all-time favorite. Think of it as the shtetl antecedent to *The Silver Palate*'s celebrated Chicken Marbella. It's a chicken cut in quarters, cooked in a pot with onions, salt, and pepper, the prunes thrown in toward the end for a sweet counterpoint, served on white rice. The last time Mom made it for me was in 2001, the year I later learned she had had her first strokes. The chicken was good, but I was both distracted and disturbed by the Minute Rice she made to go with it, instead of her own. It was chalk white and tasted vaguely synthetic, each grain standing separate and alien from the others. It was easier, she said with a shrug, annoyed I had even mentioned it. I often think of that rice and wonder why I didn't recognize it as the harbinger of disaster it was, the culinary equivalent of the mismatched buttons on my dress. What constituted chaos for me.

I kept telling myself I would try these recipes and they would be just as I remembered. Or if for some reason they weren't, I would do as Mom instructed in the note she enclosed with the folder: *My darling Alex, Here are the recipes you requested. Try them, adjust seasoning to taste, call me if these don't work. Happy, Happy Birthday! Love, Mom.*

But as the years passed, I didn't try them. I didn't want to eat them without her. Part of the power of home cooking is that everything tastes better when someone else makes it for you. But the other part is being together, sharing it. The farthest I was willing to go was to make her dishes while I had her on the phone, complaining all the while about the inaccuracy of her measurements while she just laughed. "So if you want more salt, use more salt!" she'd say. That was the closest we came to cooking together, and she still didn't find it fun.

These days, when I make her food, watching the familiar dishes take shape over the heat, smelling the signature Mom-is-home aromas that signaled safe harbor at the end of the day, it brings her nearer, yes. But even as I imagine her over my shoulder, watching me as I used to watch her, I know I am cooking alone. It is not home cooking without the home. She cooked for me because she loved me and wanted to take care of me so I would grow up to be big and strong. And I thought I had done just that, until it came time for me to take care of her.

Chicken with Prunes

1 tablespoon paprika
1 tablespoon garlic powder
1 teaspoon salt, plus more as needed
½ teaspoon freshly ground pepper, plus more as needed
1 chicken (about 4 pounds), quartered
2 medium onions, finely diced
26 pitted prunes
White rice, for serving

Place a kettle of water on high heat to bring to a boil. Meanwhile, in a small bowl, mix together the paprika, garlic powder, 1 teaspoon salt, and ½ teaspoon pepper. Thoroughly dust all sides of the chicken pieces with the mixture and set aside.

Spread the onions across the bottom of a Dutch oven or other large, deep pot with a tight-fitting lid. Arrange the chicken pieces in a single layer on top of the onions. Add boiling water until it comes halfway up the sides of the chicken, being careful not to get water on top of the chicken.

Place over high heat to bring to a boil, then reduce heat to medium-low. Cook, covered, for 45 minutes. Taste broth and adjust salt. Cook, covered, for another 15 minutes and correct for salt again. If the broth is still light yellow, increase heat and boil, uncovered, until the liquid has deepened in color, about 5 minutes.

Add prunes, submerging them in the liquid; if necessary, add just enough water to cover the prunes. Cover, reduce heat to low, and simmer for 25 minutes. Taste broth and add salt if needed. Remove from heat and set aside to cool.

Remove cooled chicken from the pan and discard skin and bones. Return the meat to the liquid with the prunes. Reheat and serve over rice.

Serves 4

Three

A fter Mom's aortobifemoral bypass surgery, it became clear she would need more help than I could give her. Her driving had gotten progressively worse, and her parking was disastrous. In the garage of her apartment building, she would invariably pull too close to a column, scratching the car's finish. One time, she scraped loose a racing stripe. It flapped in the wind, like a wayward antenna, until Dad took matters in hand and taped it back onto the door. He thought she simply wasn't paying attention and saw no need to boost his insurance premiums by having it repaired.

I started hearing on a weekly basis from my father, brimming with complaints. Every Sunday for the fifty years they had been married, Mom made him eggs, he informed me, as if I hadn't known. One weekend, he asked her to scramble them and she fried them instead. His voice shook with outrage. She was purposefully not doing what he asked, he said. I tried explaining that she actually could not remember what he asked. He hung up on me.

If Dad was in his own world of denial, Mom was right beside him. She felt there was a plot against her driving. When she told Goldstein about it, he was instantly sympathetic. Of course she should drive, he said. All she needed to do was pass a simulated driver's test. She failed it. Twice.

Dr. Weinberger referred me to Roberta Epstein, a social worker in Scarsdale who was an expert in dealing with senior citizens who did not want to be dealt with. Roberta suggested a family meeting, so we could all talk about taking care of Mom, with Mom. We listened as Roberta suggested a day-to-day division of labor, encompassing doctor's appointments and monitoring medication, that would involve me less and my siblings more. This generated more denial. Phoebe, who had a toddler, seemed incredulous that Mom had somehow become the one who required outside assistance. Emmett, who lived and worked in Texas, had an infant. He invited Mom to come and visit. Greg, with a toddler of his own, said if and when Mom needed another surgery down in the city, sure, he'd be glad to pitch in. I just stared. The three of them stared back. I was infant-and-toddler-free, with stepchildren who were in their twenties. If the meeting had had a caption at the bottom of the screen, like a scene in a Woody Allen film, it would have read, *What the hell else does she have to do?*

Roberta put me in touch with a woman who provided home care attendants; she referred me to Caroline Harrison. Caroline was Irish, in her early forties, and the mother of four children. She had been doing this kind of work for years. Since Mom was unable to keep track of her medication, Caroline bought a Mediset, organized the pills, and administered them. She drove Mom to the library and surveyed her garden with her. Four hours a day, four days a week. For the first time in months, I felt I could breathe.

In the weeks after her surgery, I would call Mom to see how she was doing. "I feel like myself again," she'd say assertively.

"That's great!" I would reply. "I am so glad."

"So I don't need this woman here."

The very fact of Caroline was a problem for Mom, striking at the heart of her stubborn independence. Mom loved to drive, but it was part of Caroline's job to drive. Mom wanted to be left alone. Caroline kept her company. Mom preferred silence. Caroline preferred conversation. Caroline is a person who is naturally patient. She never rushes. She asks how you are and when you say fine, she asks you again, because she actually wants to know.

"She talks too much," Mom complained.

"Okay, tell her that."

She sighed. And waited.

"I'm sorry, but I'm not going to tell her for you," I said. "Even though you don't want her help, you need her help, for now at least, so you're going to have to work out a relationship with her."

A week later I asked Caroline how things were going. "Just fine," she said calmly. I could tell she knew perfectly well that she was driving my mother crazy, even though my mother hadn't said a word to her. "You know, it's hard for your mom, being a college professor, not to be teaching anymore," Caroline said.

"She's an educated woman and very accomplished. It's upsetting to her not to be working."

In 1960s Passaic, Mom was the only working mother around. She taught elementary school then, but she was already earning her EdD; teaching was part of her doctoral program. I remember visiting her classroom and meeting the principal, the standard-issue stern, gray-haired woman who smiled without smiling, and the janitor, a man who laughed easily and talked to Mom for a long time.

"Everyone thinks the principal is the most important person in the school, but she's not," Mom told me. "People see her coming and they hide. The janitor is the most important because no one thinks he is. He sees everything that's going on. The people no one thinks are important are the ones you should always treat well because they actually run the place. If you're smart enough to realize that, they'll protect you every time."

Once Mom got her doctorate from Rutgers, she left the elementary school and started teaching undergraduate psychology at Newark State College. When I was twelve, we moved to Scarsdale and she landed a job at Iona College in New Rochelle, where she would stay for thirty-five years. She loved the circumscribed life of the campus, with its pretty brick buildings. The college was run by the Christian Brothers. She taught some of them pastoral counseling, which I thought was the perfect topic for a Jewish mother; who else would know better than the Church? She had some of the Brothers over to our house once, a group of shy men clustered at the far end of the living room. They each shook my hand, one by one, none of them meeting my eye. But when my mother appeared, they followed her around like ducklings.

Mostly, though, Mom taught secular psychology, undergraduate and graduate. She gloried in her classrooms, where she was both authority and character; in later years, she carried a pince-nez to read her notes from the podium. When I first saw her there—she had me corral some high school friends to take Rorschach tests, to the alarm of at least one mother—she was sharp, in charge, funny. Her students loved her and for decades generated waves of Christmas cards, filled with appreciation and thanks.

She was genuinely engaged by her subject, and she'd sit at the dining room table long after everyone was asleep, reading the latest research so she could explain it clearly. She loved teaching, tirelessly sowing the seeds for that aha moment when her students' eyes would widen and she could see them getting it. She loved work itself, a role beyond that of wife and mother.

But a working mother in the 1960s suburbs tended to arouse wariness and resentment among her nonworking peers. Once, Mom couldn't get back in time to make lunch for me and Greg—we were in elementary school then and still came home at noon. At the last minute, she arranged for our next-door neighbor to take us instead. A youngish woman, married but with no children of her own, the neighbor seemed scandalized to have been enlisted as an accessory to such careless behavior. Greg and I stood stock-still inside her doorway, hesitating to remove our coats and scarves and boots as she chattered nervously from a distance, watching without offering to help. Finally, she steered us to a table set with a white cloth where she served us peanut butter and jelly sandwiches (no crusts and, shockingly, no fun) and sat on the edge of a nearby couch, knees pressed together, a smile seared on her face. When we finished, she opened a box of candies tossed upside down in their paper cups. A white film covered most of them, but dutifully we each picked one that we ended up cradling, half eaten in our sodden palms, until we could dump them in the gutter in front of her house, no doubt in plain view. I don't remember ever seeing her again.

Then there was the time Mom arrived late to my flying-up ceremony from Brownies to Girl Scouts. I was with my troop, enmeshed in some nonsensical pageantry, but not so enmeshed that I missed the face Robin Cohen's mother made at Barbara Packer's mother when the door opened and Mom appeared. I saw my mother see it, too. She took the nearest empty seat and, ignoring them, fixed her gaze on me, blazing encouragement and excitement my way. When the ceremony was over, the very same women who had rolled their eyes at her belated entrance came over and shook her hand and congratulated me. Mom was polite to a fault.

Until I was older, I didn't understand that politeness was one of her weapons. It was Grandma, Mom's mother, who once described Mom to me as the most polite person she had ever known, a characterization I found peculiar. Not that you should be rude to your own family, but those are the people you're supposed to trust, open up to. Only later did I realize why it was Grandma to whom Mom was most polite.

Grandma, whose given name was Anna, insisted on being called Ann, which to her ear sounded more American. She had been born in the United States, after all. Her mother, Tessie, had emigrated from Italy when she was sixteen for an arranged marriage to a musician exactly twice her age. They had six children. Ann was the fifth, and among her older brothers was my mother's favorite person in the world, Selig. Like my grandmother, Selig (pronounced SEE-lig) changed his given name, though not by choice. He was Salvatore at birth, but the name got Tessie summoned to his Bronx elementary school by his third-grade teacher. Once the teacher determined that the family was indeed Jewish, she informed Tessie that Salvatore was an inappropriate name for a Jewish boy. Tessie, née Teresa, was no match for the New York City public school system, so at eight years old, Salvatore became Selig. The other siblings—Max, Lou, Ruby, and Sarah—managed to keep their names. Ruby actually grew up to marry a woman named Pearl.

When her husband's paychecks proved too few for Tessie's taste, she took in sewing to earn money of her own. She hated being beholden. This lesson imprinted early on Mom. Once she was finally out of school, she insisted that she and Dad keep separate checking accounts so her expenses would never be questioned or denied.

Tessie worked well into her later years. By the time I met her, she was in her eighties, a shrunken, birdlike woman who smiled at me and spoke to my mother. I liked sitting at her black and gold Singer sewing machine, with its intricate, wrought-iron pedal that seemed miles from my feet. As a young woman, her daughter Ann had worked, too, as a milliner. But the man Ann married, Herman, sold nylon stockings when they first came on the market and did well enough that she didn't need to return to hats. Handy as she was with a needle, she was uninterested in repeating her mother's example. She didn't work again until after Herman died, when she took a job as a receptionist in a doctor's office. I'm not sure she needed the money as much as the company. She told me that each time the door opened, she pretended it was Grandpa coming in next.

I found Grandma to be a lot of fun. She was addicted to *As the World Turns*, among other soap operas. "My stories," Grandma called them. In my entire life, I'd never seen my mother turn on the television earlier than the six o'clock news. It was a matter of principle. But Grandma loved the soaps and so did I. We'd watch them together when she came over, and later I got hooked on *Ryan's Hope* all on my own. I never did pick up Grandma's penchant for crossword puzzles, and she wasn't much of a cook, although her meatballs in Ragú spaghetti sauce weren't too bad. But she loved to shop, go out to eat, play cards and mah-jongg. And she taught me important things, like how to tap all around my eyes with my fourth finger to lessen the bags—I would need to know that when I grew up, she said. We watched *White Christmas* together every year when she came to stay for the holidays.

She sewed patches on my jeans in the style of the day. Once, she even jumped rope with me.

It's true I wasn't as close to her as I was with Nana, my other grandmother, but Grandma lived in the Bronx, so I didn't see her as often. I knew that Dad and Grandma never got along— whatever she would do or say, he would invariably sneer "low class" behind her back. When she came to visit, he'd make himself scarce. Mom made herself scarce, too, but in the aftermath, her always sensitive stomach would blow up anyway and she would eat Maalox by the fistful.

The only problem I ever encountered with Grandma was with her bookshelves, which were stocked exclusively with Reader's Digest abridgments of great books. The spines were adorned with curly gold letters that were hard to read; side by side they looked like wallpaper. Once when I was nine or ten, I visited her solo for a sleepover, and she tried urging *The Last of the Mohicans* on me. Undoubtedly, Mom had told her that I loved to read. But I was a regular at the public library by then, and the idea of a book being "abridged" aroused deep suspicion. Why? I demanded. What was cut out? Who made that decision? What if I missed a crucial detail of the story? I had been trained by the master, after all. Abridged might just as well mean amputated.

Though Grandma was somewhat disconcerted by this inter- rogation, I managed to redeem myself. That night, I slept next to her, and when I woke up in the morning, she beamed at me. "You were so quiet," she said. "I didn't even hear you breathe." That was a big compliment for Grandma, who was no fan of bodily functions, or bodies in general. A story about her kindergarten days was famous in our family. The teacher told the children to gather in a circle in the middle of the room and join hands. But Grandma refused to take the outstretched hand of the little boy next to her. He was dirty, she announced. She didn't want to touch him. She made him go stand next to someone else. When we were growing up, we all found this story funny. Picky, persnickety Grandma, even then!

Mom never laughed.

Barbara Goldfein, my mother, was Grandma's oldest child and only daughter. She was born healthy in the Bronx in 1931. When she was three, she contracted polio in the municipal pool where Grandma brought her to cool off on a summer's day. Mom spent months in the hospital in quarantine; not even her parents were allowed to visit. She required follow-up surgeries until she was a teenager. In the periods when she was bedridden, she would listen to a small transistor radio, placed on the pillow beside her, a link to the outside world. This was a gift from her beloved uncle Selig, who had no children of his own. Selig, who was an architect, always looked past her illness and treated her as herself, the lively girl for whom he had felt an affinity from the start. More than anything else, I believe, it was a combination of the radio on the pillow and the encouragement from an accomplished, educated man that propelled her in later years, up out of that bed and into the world. I knew Selig only when he was quite elderly, but the expression on his face whenever he saw my mother was the most delicious combination of proud, admiring, and downright tickled.

Grandma, however, was never quite able to forgive her daughter for getting sick, for having one foot smaller than the other. My mother's deformity was a constant reminder of her own mistake, which, however innocent, was indelible. Grandma had been plagued by her own flat feet since she was a child. They caused her terrible pain and necessitated her wearing iron arches in her shoes. She used to tell how her eldest brother, Max, would order her down six flights of stairs to buy him candy, timing her all the way there and back. She'd slam one hand into another as she would tell this story to accentuate each blow of foot against arch. She hobbled more than walked, and Selig used to call her Minnie Mouse. Years later, when she came with our family to Israel, she stayed outside the Mosque of Omar rather than remove her shoes. She was concerned about the other visitors scrutinizing her bunions, or her corns, I forget which. I don't think I've ever seen Mom that mad. "We traveled halfway around the world and all she can think about is her feet!" she fumed. "Who cares?"

If their feet were one battleground, their faces were another. Grandma had a movie-star face: heart-shaped with a porcelain complexion, sea-green eyes, jet-black hair, and a deep red mouth. That she was five feet tall and weighed 180 pounds never got in the way of her conception of herself as a great beauty, which she was. Mom's prominent jaw and cheekbones and wide-spaced brown eyes were not enough to distract from her slightly buck teeth and large-pored skin. She was not perfect. Mom said Grandma always made her feel ugly, found something to criticize in the way she looked or what she wore. "Nothing is ever enough for her," she fretted for as long as Grandma was alive.

As Grandma got older, her hair remained black save for a perfect white stripe that grew in at the front. She kept her looks. In later years, her outfits were based on black pants that melded seamlessly with her orthopedic shoes, but she stockpiled beautiful blouses for day and evening. She remarried, to a nice old man who interested me not at all. Grandma told me she liked him because his feet were pink and clean. The girl had a theme.

For her part, Mom plowed all of her energy and resources into her brain, studying like crazy and excelling at school. Not that she was lacking socially. She was authentically beautiful, no matter what Grandma thought, and had dates before dinner, for dinner, and after dinner. Her feet notwithstanding, she loved to dance. She wanted to become a nurse, but Grandma forbade it, recoiling from any profession based on bedpans and germs. Her idea was for Mom to drop out of high school at sixteen to marry Izzy Twersky, the rabbi's son. That way she could be respectable without calling too much attention to herself. But the allure of a living-room suite—couch, love seat, and coffee table—that so captivated Grandma escaped Mom completely, and she escaped Izzy Twersky. The struggle between them, with Grandma pushing her to be "normal" while Mom defied her at every turn, went on for decades.

At the University of Wisconsin, Mom was drawn to bio-chemistry, but the department head steered her to psychology.

Biochemistry, he informed her, was an "inappropriate" field for women. Mom stayed there for only a year; her father ran out of money. She came home and graduated from NYU; she was earning her master's there when, through a mutual friend, she met my father.

Unlike my mother, my father was an immigrant. His father, Gregory, came from a family of tenant farmers in Poland, but by the time he settled in Passaic, Gregory had somehow become Harry and gone to work as a peddler, selling fruits and vegetables from a horse and wagon. In 1929, he sent for his wife, Rose, to join him, with my father and his older sister, Evelyn.

Eventually Harry and Rose opened a store, Cut-Rate Fruits and Vegetables. They had a third child, Marcia, and the family lived at the rear of the store, the parents in one bedroom, the two girls in the other. Dad slept on a cot in the dining area.

His father, whom he mentioned rarely and seemed to despise, died young, leaving him to support a mother and younger sister. He had enough shame about his background to hide it; in later years he spun tall tales about his family's royal lineage in Russia or Germany or Alsace. There were also accounts of distant relatives meeting historical figures—Napoléon Bonaparte was one—when it seemed more likely that he had (possibly) been glimpsed in a parade.

But the details of my father's childhood remain sketchy to me, because he never wanted to talk about them. The best way for me to intuit what it was like is to recount an incident from my own childhood: I wanted to buy my father a Chanukah gift. Mom took me to Wechsler's, the upscale department store in Passaic, where we bought our dress-up clothes. I saw a soft slate blue scarf, a flat, elegant wool, and fell in love. When my father opened the box, he pulled out the scarf for closer examination before throwing it down. "No one on Wall Street wears scarves like this," he informed me. "They need to be silk on one side, cashmere on the other." I returned the scarf. I was seven at the time.

What I did understand about my father's childhood was that he felt constant pressure to pull rabbits out of hats and make things right: make enough money to put Marcia through college, make enough money for his mother to feel secure. He worked maniacally. For him, the library was comfort and escape. His love of history—names, dates, places—occupied him the way sports did other men. He could tell you every last detail about the War of 1812, but few from his youth.

When Harry died of a brain tumor at fifty-two, Nana closed Cut-Rate Fruits and Vegetables, and Dad enlisted in the Air Force. When the war ended, he enrolled at the University of Missouri on the GI Bill, earning a bachelor's degree in journalism and a master's in history. He returned to New York, where he worked as a writer and editor at a number of magazines before settling on a career in corporate public relations. He also owned a printing company that produced and mailed press releases and annual reports.

In many ways, he and Mom were perfect for each other. Here was a woman devoted, as he was, to the life of the mind. For her, too, the library was comfort and escape—from the limitations of being a woman, and from having two differently sized and shaped feet and a bum leg. The science of behavior, contained on the page, made sense to her in a way that people's actual behavior didn't quite.

My mother had always felt odd, misshapen, out of place. She sensed that my father, running from his circumstances and emotions, felt the same. She could make him a home, give him shelter and companionship and partnership. Maybe he wouldn't have to be the only one making miracles all the time. Maybe she could make some, too. He believed in her.

As did his mother. Nana not only championed my mother's ambitions, but made it possible for her to fulfill them. In my mother, she saw the possibility for a life and career she never could have dreamed of for herself. Born and raised in Bialystok, which was Russia before World War I and Poland after it, Nana had a facility for languages—she could speak seven of them. This came in handy for her job, working in a store selling women's coats to Russians, Poles, and Germans.

Once she landed in Passaic, the fruit and vegetable store was a step down, grindingly hard work. Yet Nana managed to cultivate her many interests. She read the *Forward* in Yiddish but taught herself enough English to subscribe to both *The New Yorker* and *The New York Times*. She was a lifelong opera fan; I listened to WQXR with her every Saturday afternoon, to the Texaco-sponsored live broadcasts from the Met. In her younger years, the Yiddish theater was still vibrant, and she loved going to it on

Second Avenue in Manhattan. When it waned, she took to Broadway. She also loved the movies, anything with Bette Davis or Barbara Stanwyck, strong women. It just so happened that Mom had been named for Barbara Stanwyck—Nana and Grandma had that much in common. But the similarities seemed to stop there. When Mom told her own mother that she was pursuing a doctorate, Grandma was dumbfounded. What did she need *that* for? She was already married, with small children, for heaven's sake.

But the way Nana saw it was that if she, for all her intelligence, had to settle for selling coats and cucumbers, the most constructive thing she could do would be to help her serious daughter-in-law earn the highest academic degree possible. So every weekend, for years, Dad dropped Greg and me at her house. For two precious days each week, Nana relieved Mom of cooking and caring for us so that she could work toward her doctorate uninterrupted.

Nana was a tall, imposing woman who would take me firmly in hand as she strode, unafraid, into the squawking, stinking live poultry market that was still in existence in Passaic. Everything about her seemed big—hands, feet, arms so much longer than Mom's. She was a comforting presence, in daylight, at least. If I had trouble sleeping and started to cry, she'd sit with me at the kitchen table with all the lights on, and boy was I sorry then. By that point she had taken her teeth out for the night. There they were, near the sink in one of those glasses that used to be a Breakstone's sour cream container. Her face, which seemed like one on Mount Rushmore to me, had lost half its heft. I was more afraid of that than the dark.

She was an expert cook, and I spent hours watching her. She always found a task for me. When she made chopped liver, she would screw a cast-iron grinder onto the edge of the kitchen table and let me turn the handle as she fed the livers into it. We would sit in her living room in front of a small black-and-white TV to watch Julia Child. Just us cooks.

I was crazy about Nana and I was crazy about Dad's sister, Evelyn, who lived in Manhattan, where she worked as an executive secretary. I named her Kiki after she pretended to be a monster who made noises that sounded like *khee-khee*. She would turn up on many of those weekends when Nana took care of us, to paint my fingernails and read me my favorite book, *The Party Pig*. When I visited her in the city, she was a Doris Day movie come to life, living in a studio apartment with a cute little kitchen, surrounded by neighbors who popped in and out. Every Christmas she would take me to see the windows at Saks Fifth Avenue, then to lunch. She lived a glamorous life, I thought, and as I grew up that held true. When I was thirteen, she successfully lobbied Mom for permission to take me to see *Hair* on Broadway in spite of the notorious nude scene. When I was at camp, she wrote me long funny letters about the people in her office, then about meeting friends at restaurants with romantic names like Patricia Murphy's Candlelight Restaurant.

When it came to food, though, Nana's house was good enough for me. My two favorite dishes of hers were fried meat kreplach and potato latkes. The latkes were spectacular, crispy on the outside, tender inside, never greasy. The real marvel was that the centers stayed white and never oxidized. After dinner, Nana and I would sit at the kitchen table together, she with a glass of tea and a sugar cube in her mouth, me with a glass of milk and a Tootsie Roll in mine so each mouthful would taste like chocolate. I was so happy I even forgot about Mom being so busy.

Because of Nana, Mom was at a disadvantage in the kitchen from the start. No matter how well she did, Dad always preferred Nana's cooking. It was never a fair match, and most of the time Mom didn't even try to compete. When Nana made gefilte fish, she started with live carp in the bathtub. Mom started—and ended—with a jar from the supermarket. She was a modern woman who embraced convenience.

Marrying my father meant that Mom had to learn to keep a kosher household (though outside the house, she, and we, ate what we pleased). That was okay with her; she valued rules. In fact, Grandma's more casual approach to life seemed to repel her—maybe she felt that with a little more vigilance, a certain swimming pool might have been avoided, at the very least. The built-in limitations Mom married into—no mixing meat and dairy, no pork or shellfish—had their own perverse appeal. For all the dynamism she had summoned in her younger years to get up out of her bed and move forward in her life, she took a contrary comfort in being told she couldn't do certain things. I think it provided relief to realize that there were actual limits in life and she didn't have to do *everything*. But it was also wrapped up with not deserving—the idea that because she was just as imperfect as Grandma perceived her, freedom of choice could not be hers.

No matter how hard Mom worked, at school or at home, she never expected anyone to give her credit, and when someone did, it surprised her. Then it seemed to scare her. She found social attention unnerving. My father would hold forth with company while my mother smoked and listened, served and cleared. She was allergic to anyone asking her personal questions; she had a particular aversion to "everyone knowing my business." When her schedule allowed and she came to pick me up from Brownies or ballet, the other mothers would gather on the sidewalk, chatting. She stayed in the car, behind the wheel, head down, reading. This woman who had overcome so much tended to see certain situations as potentially fraught, whether they were or not.

Privacy was the twin to politeness. Mom never snooped through her children's drawers, never opened her husband's mail. And she demanded the same of us. We were never to be in her bedroom without her. She abhorred gossip, or even ordinary small talk. She answered neighbors' questions courteously and as briefly as possible. It took me years to realize that her extreme stance on privacy was linked to shame, specifically shame related to the physical or medical.

I recall being shocked when the director of a community theater production in which I appeared, having met my mother, branded her "an ice queen." Years later, though, I smiled in recognition when my longtime shrink dubbed my mother's acerbic assessments of people "Barb's barbs." I loved them because they were dead-on accurate, and her schoolmarm delivery, that prim politesse as her cover, made them even funnier. She never cursed, though. That was a sucker's way out, one I took every time. But she built a moat early on, and she fired across it, from the least likely of angles.

Roberta Epstein came to see Mom once a week. She agreed with Caroline about my mother missing her job. "She's mourning the loss of her professional life," she said. "She was a teacher for fifty-two out of seventy-four years. Besides the illness, this is another way she's no longer the same person." She asked about Mom's friends. I told her that though my mother had dinner a few times a year with colleagues in the psychology department, she really hadn't had many close friends.

An exception was Sister Jeanette, a nun who was something of a radical when Mom met her in 1970; she was among those who successfully challenged the Church's mandate on wearing the habit. She was a fiercely intelligent woman, independent within the strictures of her chosen life, who I think appreciated finding a sister spirit of sorts in Mom. Once or twice she even arranged for Mom to go on retreat with her to a convent in Connecticut. I suspect that for Mom, part of the appeal might have been solace, that compared with Sister Jeanette, her own life had finally come to resemble the long-elusive "normal."

But nothing resembled any iteration of normal now. The professional life that had sustained my mother for so long was gone. Goldstein tested her for Alzheimer's. She didn't have it, which was good news, he said. Stroke-related dementia was not progressive in the same way as Alzheimer's. Still, she continued to deteriorate. A few months later, Caroline called with a problem. Whenever she and Mom went to the cash machine, Caroline would stand back to give her privacy. Now Mom was stopping halfway through the process and leaving empty-handed. She couldn't remember which buttons to push. Loss of executive function, Goldstein said. Which was a fancy way of saying that she could no longer manage the progression of a task, follow a prompt. Everyone in the family kept calling me, asking when Mom would get better. Soon, I assured them, blinded by denial of my own. Soon.

Goldstein had three goals for Mom's care: to keep her depression at bay, to enhance her cognitive skills, and to stimulate her concentration without making her too anxious. Next to this, parting the Red Sea was child's play. At one point, Mom was so scattered and unable to focus that he prescribed Ritalin. Two weeks later, it kicked in. She called me, screaming and crying. She couldn't read, she couldn't concentrate, she couldn't sit still. She had somehow managed to wait until Caroline had gone for the day before calling me. She preferred to lose her mind without an audience, thank you.

I put her on hold, leaving Goldstein frantic messages from the other line. When I clicked back, she was still screaming, and as I tried placating her, there came a lull. "This is not me, it's the medication," she said clearly, authoritatively. I almost cried. In the midst of this nightmare, my mom had appeared to help me, to explain. As she always had. Goldstein called back, genuinely disconcerted. Good-bye, Ritalin. I started to learn the long, hard lesson that when it comes to medication, less can be more.

Not that I wanted to learn. Like everyone else, I ached to be done with this. But I wasn't as interested in moving forward as I was in moving backward. I wanted a do-over. When I asked Weinberger if the strokes were diet-related, he shook his head. Smoking, he said. But Grandma had the same strokes and she never smoked. When I vented my frustration to a friend, she said, "Doctors have no idea what causes this. It's completely random. Some people get it, some people don't, and they have no idea why. They just won't admit it."

All I wanted was magic—the perfect recipe that would make Mom better, sane, herself again. But while Goldstein continued to tweak and trade her medications regularly, the ideal balance remained elusive.

In search of stability, I returned to the kitchen. Ah, my mother's roast chicken. Sinfully easy, career-woman chicken. It reminded me why its dynamic duo of Lawry's Seasoned Salt and garlic powder was the kitchen crack of 1957. I had long used the mixture on lamb chops, one of Nat's and Simon's favorite dishes, as it had always been one of mine. Mom rubbed the combination on a chicken, stuffed it with an onion cut in quarters, and placed it in a roasting pan on top of another onion, sliced. She poured in some water, cooked it covered for an hour, uncovered for half an hour or so, and voilà, brown on top and moist on the bottom.

There was my magic: The chicken worked, every time. I could barely stand to go a week without making it. I got the idea of pairing it with latkes—Mom's latkes as she had learned them from Nana—and serving them to Arthur and Barbara Gelb, friends of mine and Frank's who were both in their eighties, still going strong. Arthur had been the managing editor of *The New York Times* for years and a mentor to Frank. To both of us he was also a fantasy daddy, the kind of man who says "I love you" as easily as "Good morning," who calls when a piece of yours is published and tells you at great length exactly why you are a genius. Barbara, more reserved, like my own Barbara, listened to me talk about Mom's travails one night at dinner and, as I spoke, leaned over and wordlessly stroked my hair. I practically dissolved on the floor. Their friendship nourished me.

My fascination with cooking my mother's food struck a particular chord with Arthur; he had also grown up in the Bronx and loved his own mother's cooking. "She made the best latkes," he told me.

"Mine are pretty good," I said. "You should try them."

They came to dinner. I worried that the latkes wouldn't be good enough, but after one bite, Arthur was rapturous: "Exactly the same as my mother's!" He went on and on about their perfection, crispy on the outside, tender on the inside. They liked the roast chicken fine. Or at least Barbara did. "Don't worry about the chicken next time," Arthur instructed. "Just make the latkes."

Toward the end of that year, I wrote a column for the *Times* about making latkes for Arthur, the joy it gave him and the joy it gave me to re-create a dish from a mother long gone. I barely realized what I was doing. I wrote that I had time-traveled to a Bronx kitchen in the 1930s. I didn't connect it to the Scarsdale kitchen of the 1970s with the wallpaper crisscrossed with roses, where my mom turned out latke batter in a pre-Cuisinart blender.

After the column ran, I got a call from *The Martha Stewart Show*. They wanted me to come on and make the latkes. What an unexpected lift! When I told Mom that her latkes were about to become world-famous, she was bursting with pride. If only Nana were here, we said to each other. She and Caroline planned to watch it together. Arthur and Barbara planned to watch it together, too.

I got to the studio early but did not meet Martha Stewart until right before my segment. She was tall—maybe even taller than Nana—and somewhat chilly. The cameras rolled, and I explained that my eighty-two-year-old friend Arthur loved my latkes because they reminded him of his mom, whom he missed. The audience broke into a spontaneous "Oh!" and I stopped being nervous.

When it was over, I called Frank from the dressing room to see how it had gone. He told me that at exactly ten a.m., when the show was to start, President Bush made an unscheduled televised speech. He was still speaking, in fact. The show never aired.

I asked the producers for a DVD. I promised Mom we would watch it together, but she never asked about it again. She had forgotten.

Roast Chicken

1 whole chicken, about 4 pounds
2 medium onions
Garlic powder
Lawry's Seasoned Salt
1 cup water

Preheat oven to 350°F.

Rinse the chicken and pat dry with paper towels. Slice one onion and distribute rings in a layer in a pan large enough to hold the chicken. Sprinkle chicken liberally with garlic powder, then with the Lawry's Seasoned Salt. Cut the second onion in quarters and stuff it inside the chicken, then place chicken on top of the layer of onion rings, breast side up.

Add ¾ cup water to the pan, cover, and roast for 1 hour.

Uncover, baste, and add remaining ¼ cup water. Return to oven and cook 45 minutes more, or until well browned.

Serves 4

Potato Latkes

Tip from Nana: Grate the onion and potato together to avoid oxidization and keep the batter white. It works!

> 2 large eggs
> All-purpose white potatoes, peeled and grated to make
>   3 cups, packed
> 1/4 cup grated onion (see headnote)
> I teaspoon salt, or more to taste
> 1/4 teaspoon ground pepper
> 2–4 tablespoons matzo meal, as needed
> Canola oil, for frying
> Applesauce or sour cream, for serving (optional)

In a large mixing bowl, beat eggs lightly. Add potatoes, onion, salt, and pepper, and mix well. Stir in 2 tablespoons matzo meal and let sit about 30 seconds to absorb moisture in batter. If necessary, add additional matzo meal to make a thick, wet batter. Taste for seasoning and adjust.

Place a large skillet over medium heat and add 3 tablespoons canola oil. When oil is hot, drop in heaping 1/8-cupfuls (about 2 tablespoons) of batter, flattening them gently to make thick pancakes. When bottoms have browned, after 2 to 3 minutes, flip and brown on other side. Drain on paper towels and sprinkle with additional salt to taste. Keep cooked pancakes warm on a baking sheet in the oven, and add oil to the skillet between batches as needed. Use two skillets for faster cooking, especially if doubling or tripling the recipe.

Serve hot, with applesauce or sour cream if desired.

Makes about 40 pancakes

Four

· ● · · · · ·

A s soon as I could read, I became transfixed by a thick book Mom kept in her kitchen and I now keep in mine: *Modern Encyclopedia of Cooking.* It begins with a year's worth of daily menus for Breakfast, Luncheon, and Dinner, except on Sundays, when Luncheon is replaced by Supper.

Here is the bill of fare for the first Tuesday in April:

Breakfast: Stewed Prunes, Griddle Cakes, Syrup, Beverages.

Lunch: Green Beans With Onions and Bacon, Head Lettuce, French Dressing, Whole Wheat Bread, Butter, Stewed Rhubarb, Cocoa.

Dinner: Beef Turnovers, Buttered Carrots, Tomato Aspic Salad, Bread, Butter, Sliced Bananas in Orange Juice, Beverages.

The recipes, of course, are all contained within the book. At the bottom of each page of menus is a piece of housewifely wisdom. On this particular page it reads, *Prunes have moved from boardinghouse to penthouse status.*

Well! A breakfast in the penthouse, something French for

lunch, and aspic for dinner. It sounded like a Fred Astaire–Ginger Rogers movie to me. I surely was conflating aspic with Mary Astor, ignoring that it was somehow related to the gelatinous lumps that clung to gefilte fish, which I would firmly scrape to the side of my plate. But the message was clear: Food was occasion, celebration, whether high or low. I knew that even snacktime in school, where we got two plain graham crackers and a container of milk, was a happier ten minutes than math.

In our house, the occasions we celebrated were usually Jewish holidays. I knew there were Jewish families who bought Christmas trees and called them Chanukah bushes, just for fun, but my family was not one of them. When Dad first came to the United States, he'd felt the excitement of Christmas all around him and been inspired to join in. He hung a stocking of his own—and his father filled it with a lump of coal.

So we stuck to Passover and Thanksgiving and Chanukah. After Nana died, we often traveled to Wyncote, Pennsylvania, to celebrate with Aunt Marcia, Dad's younger sister, her husband, Bernie, and my cousins Roberta and David. There I encountered a most vexing creation, one heartily endorsed by Dad: the children's table. From the heirs to Cut-Rate Fruits and Vegetables, this was either a grand affectation, an expression of not-so-veiled hostility, or both. To be quarantined at a separate table in the corner was, for a kid like me who watched grown-ups the way other kids watched television, the equivalent of being sent to a penal colony.

Eventually a circular table was appended to the end of the rectangular adult table, and we four children sat near, though at a distinct remove from, the adults. Even Kiki, my fun aunt, with no husband or kids of her own to distract her, was completely barricaded. I was admonished frequently to keep my seat.

But one year Aunt Marcia made a Baked Alaska, a dessert people ate on cruise ships and at the Waldorf-Astoria, that's how rich and sophisticated it was. Not to mention difficult to make. When she carried it out of the kitchen, having set a match to it, I could not keep my seat. I dashed behind Mom's chair to get a better look. No one even yelled at me, it was that momentous an occasion. Delicious, too, as I recall, the ice cream remaining magically intact beneath its flaming cloak of meringue.

As an event, it almost rivaled the excitement of the Jewish War Veterans conventions my family attended in the Catskills, occasions even more special than holidays. Each year in the fall and again in the late spring, I was the first one in my class out the door when the school bell rang on the designated Friday afternoon. Dad had left work early to pick up Mom, then Greg and me, and off we'd go.

When we arrived at the appointed hotel—the Concord, Grossinger's, or Brown's—Mom would invariably succumb to some sort of packing-induced headache, break her own rules, and gratefully lie down. Dad would take Greg and me downstairs to explore the hotel. We would locate the pinball machines—a highlight of our evenings—then find the ice-skating rink, empty and dark, which we'd revisit on Saturday morning. A long walk down another hallway and we'd smell chlorine from the indoor pool before seeing the glass walls enclosing it. The final point of interest was the gift shop, a place to visit all weekend long, where I would zero in on a doll I had a fifty-fifty shot at getting, depending on the sharpness of Mom's negotiating skills, by the Sunday post-brunch departure.

After the hotel tour, we would head back upstairs, where Mom had pulled herself together, and we would all get dressed for dinner. Friday nights were semiformal; Saturday nights, formal. Mom and I would position ourselves in the lobby before dinner started and watch the women make their entrances. The fashion parade was dazzling. Turquoise chiffon, powder-pink feather boas, emerald-green satin—that last would be Mom. A dress with a small waist, a full skirt, and a wide V neckline that reached to the outer edges of her shoulders and clung there in little peaks. To me, her matching emerald green satin pumps made it the perfect outfit.

Of course, she was the prettiest one, with her Jackie bubble of black hair and red lips. We sat together right near the entrance to the dining room, like two birds on a bough, heads bent toward each other, chattering both our judgments and our delight at the procession before us. To me, each one was beautiful, even the old suntanned ladies from Florida with lipstick leaching onto their teeth, their wrinkled arms displayed proudly in the sleeveless dresses Mom proclaimed "*much* too young for them." I was too delighted by red patent leather shoes, gold lamé bags, and Empire waists studded with rhinestones to notice. The air was perfumed with excitement and anticipation—the whole weekend lay ahead!

There were usually half a dozen entrée choices for dinner, but we always got roast chicken on Friday nights—it was Shabbos after all. On Saturday night, the best choice was a rib-eye steak with French fries. While the adults sat at the table, eating forever, it seemed, Greg and I were given coins and dispatched to play pinball. We saved enough to choose two songs each from the jukebox, which, even though it was the mid-sixties and you could play "Oh, Pretty Woman," still sported a picture of Eddie Fisher and Debbie Reynolds.

Then there was the nightclub where I was allowed to sit at the table with the grown-ups and order a Flamingo, a tall pink drink in a frosted glass. My parents used to tease me about holding my eyelids open so I'd be awake by the time the show started, but the preshow dancing was entertainment in itself—the women in their flamboyant costumes, swishing their skirts, while the husbands plodded backward and forward, eyes cast down, looking bashful.

Every detail of those weekends was infused with glamour for me. When Totie Fields was booked as a headliner, I didn't think of her as a Jewish comedienne entertaining a Jewish crowd. I thought of her as a comic star, someone I had actually seen on *The Ed Sullivan Show*. When Mom ate eggs Florentine for lunch on Saturday, I didn't see two poached eggs on a bed of spinach. I saw the cobblestone streets of Italy. She never poached eggs at home, so they were as exotic to me as Baked Alaska. Sitting tall by my mother's side, I gloried in the scope of the world and all its possibilities.

The year leading up to Mom's graduation was tumultuous in our house. Before she could get her degree—in later years she'd refer to it as her fifth child—she had to finish her dissertation and defend it, and she worked desperately hard. When she served my beloved meat loaf for dinner three nights in a row, I couldn't believe my good fortune. Dad, on the other hand, was furious. He was supportive of the larger goal, yes, but in the short term there was lots of yelling. One night she practiced some of her presentation in front of the television set, clutching her papers in her hands. She spoke in a formal voice, her eyes focused on some point far past us.

"You were great!" I shouted when she was done.

"No, you weren't," Dad said.

Another fight ensued. They seemed to occur daily.

One afternoon, Mom gathered Greg and me together after Dad slammed out of the house. "That's it," she said. "We are leaving and never coming back." Her eyes glittered with anger and excitement.

Really? As long as I was going, too, that sounded thrilling. So where would we live now? Would we still have to go to school? There might have been mention of a Manhattan hotel, summoning visions of women in ball gowns and trays of champagne flutes. But wherever she was going, I was with her, all the way.

Mom put us in the car and off we went—to the movies. Then we stopped at Pompeii Pizza, where Greg and I got our usual slices and Cokes and two songs apiece on the jukebox. When we climbed back into the car, night was falling. The dashboard lighter glowed red in the dark before it hit the tip of Mom's cigarette.

"Where are we going now?" I asked, giddy with anticipation.

She kept her eyes on the road. "Home," she said.

"To our new house?"

"No." She took a deep drag. "To the house we live in."

"But I thought we were never going back!"

The fizz of her defiance had dissipated, and there she was, a tired mom with two small children who needed to be bathed and put to bed. Her sense of defeat was palpable. I was torn between disappointment and sympathy. She looked so sad.

We pulled into the driveway. The house was dark; no one was home. It seemed that Dad had missed our insurrection entirely. We went inside and, subdued, enacted the mundane business of getting ready for bed. Mom continued to avoid my eye, and I didn't push it. We both knew why.

She had lied.

Of course my mother graduated, and my parents threw a huge party in our backyard. I was almost seven, and Greg was four. People were jammed into the edges of Mom's flower garden, lined up at the brick barbecue where Dad presided. Picnic tables were covered in plaid cloths, and cans of Pabst Blue Ribbon beer covered every possible surface, including the steps to the back porch.

Mom wasn't the only one celebrating a success; Dad had found a new job on Madison Avenue that paid enough for us to move out of the Terhune Avenue starter house—farewell, Pashmans!—into a trophy house on Ridge Avenue. It was of modern design, split into three levels with a "rec room" at the bottom featuring a working fireplace. To my eye, it seemed the perfect place for a party.

Around the time of my love affair with the *Modern Encyclopedia of Cooking*, I learned somehow about the idea of caravan dinner parties, where the appetizers were served in one house, the entrées in a second, and the dessert in a third. This sounded exciting to me, and I tried persuading Mom to host one. But collaborating on entertaining did not strike her as fun. "Who wants to have to get up and put on your coat and go traipsing through the streets just as you're getting comfortable?" she sniffed.

Me, that's who.

Mom actually entertained beautifully, with way too much food and linens and flowers and crystal dishes filled with chocolates. But entertaining continued to be a rarity now that she was teaching full-time. My parents still didn't operate as a unit as often as they operated alone. While my mother was studying for her degree, she and Dad established somewhat parallel lives. She stayed home while he'd be out and about—to Nana's, to the synagogue on Saturdays, to the Jewish War Veterans meetings on Sundays. He was a big deal there, working to help get veterans their benefits. He was a big deal in Passaic, too; it was his hometown and he knew everyone. Once he was earning more money, he displayed a confidence he hadn't had before. He'd bought Mom some beautiful jewelry, and he encouraged her to wear it to one of the Jewish War Veterans conventions. No rhine-stones for her, but a double strand of pearls with matching ear-rings and a small diamond suspended on a platinum chain. Plenty of oohs and aahs from the other ladies, stifled screams from Mom once we were home and she realized she'd left it all in the dresser drawer of the hotel room.

Dad called the hotel. While they checked for the jewelry, Mom sobbed and Dad, channeling his inner statesman, or rabbi, sat us all down at the kitchen table. "The important thing to remember about something like jewelry is that it can always be replaced," he said. "To lose a thing is not a tragedy. To lose a life is a tragedy." Possessions are never as valuable as people, he assured us. You could always make more money.

It was one of his finest moments, and his theory, fortunately, was not put to the test: The jewelry was found.

But that kind of expansiveness, at home at least, was rare, and sometimes he seemed intolerant, almost disdainful of my mother. At a seder at Nana's house, as we went around the table reading from the Haggadah, someone—me? Greg?—read the words "the Eternal" as "the Internal." Mom started to laugh and could not stop. She laughed until she gasped for air and tears ran down her cheeks, but the minute she started to compose herself, she would catch sight of one of us and start all over again. The reli-gious proceedings had ground to a complete halt, and grown-up eyebrows around the table were raised meaningfully at her empty wineglass. Finally, Dad slammed his hand down on the table and made her stop.

I believe that he was proud of my mother and her accomplishments, but sometimes the pride seemed double-edged. At some temple event in a banquet hall—it must have been yet another seder—someone from each table stood to introduce the other well-dressed occupants. When it was our turn, my father got up. Unlike the other men, who started with their wives, he introduced everyone else before ending with "And last, of course, my wife." He said it like a joke, so I laughed, as a few other people did. Mostly, though, there was a rumble of disapproval. Mom looked mortified, and a while later, she got up and left. I found her outside in the hallway, smoking, at a time when smoking at the table was not only allowed but expected. I could feel her fury at ten paces.

And yet he continued to urge her on professionally, even after she gave birth to Phoebe, three years after getting her doctorate. She ran for president of the Passaic Board of Education, and he seemed to flourish in the role of campaign manager and adviser. He'd known the mayor and the rest of the relevant cast of characters for decades, and he seemed to realize that his own forays into public speaking—"And last, of course, my wife"—were not the stuff that political careers were made of. Mom not only won the election but seemed to bloom in her new role. Her armor of politeness played well in public, and her advanced degree gave her an edge of gravitas over her male opponents. She'd traded her cat-eye glasses for contact lenses and gotten a fall from the hairdresser, a clump of black corkscrew curls that she fastened onto the back of her head for special occasions, which made her look glamorous.

She became a local celebrity: Her picture was in the Passaic papers, and the phone never stopped ringing.

The bad news was that Nana had leukemia. When we'd moved to Ridge Avenue, Dad moved Nana, too, to an enclave of garden apartments, where she'd let me and Greg stay up on Saturday nights to watch *The Jackie Gleason Show* and made us bologna sandwiches as snacks even though we'd finished dinner only an hour earlier. She'd promised to teach me how to speak Yiddish, but no sooner had I started taking notes than she got sick. The last time I saw her, she was being helped out of her bedroom by Dad and Kiki. She recoiled at the brightness of the living room, but then she saw me and mustered a smile. "I know you like light on the subject," she said.

Her death made the distance between my parents' separate tracks feel especially bleak. Now Mom was never home. Classes, meetings, breakfasts in the early mornings and open houses in the evenings—she was on the job and on the town. More and more, even on weekends, Greg and I were home alone with Dad and baby Phoebe. Losing Nana had proved devastating for Dad, and he seemed withdrawn, preoccupied. Like her, Dad listened to the Texaco broadcasts from the Met, but unlike her he tended to ignore us, alternating between the newspaper and a book as he listened, never looking up. He was often curt and abrupt.

One weekend afternoon, Mom was out yet again and Greg and I were in the backyard with Dad. He was wrestling with a tree branch at the rear of the yard when the phone started to ring. Even though I was on the patio, nearer the back door, I figured he would answer it; it was probably Mom calling for a quick strategy session before whatever meeting she was about to attend. But he kept at the branch, so I got up instead and started toward the house.

"Oh, that's so nice of you to answer the phone, don't rush, take your time," he called out. His tone was so unexpectedly loving and kind that I turned, smiling, to acknowledge it. What I saw froze me in place. His face was twisted with rage and—could it be?—hatred. He looked like he wanted to split me in two. In a haze of fear and humiliation—why was I suddenly doing everything wrong, no matter how hard I tried to get it right?—I made it to the phone in time. I leaned out the screen door to announce the caller's name, and once he started toward the house, I fled.

On the occasions that Mom was home, she seemed distracted, too. One day, I was in the living room, practicing on the new piano. My lessons were a colossal waste of time and money since I had no aptitude at all. Mom was in the kitchen washing dishes, and Phoebe was strapped into a car seat that Mom had placed on the kitchen table. Phoebe had recently taken to kicking, and that little leg packed some power. There came a crash, followed by terrible screaming. Phoebe had catapulted herself off the table, landing facedown on the floor.

I ran into the kitchen, horrified. Mom picked her up, unstrapped her, soothed her as she cried. But she didn't seem sorry, as far as I could see. She seemed worn out and annoyed. I went back to the living room but bypassed the piano, curling into a ball on the cream-colored carpet, feeling like I was going to faint. The safety of Nana's house, the milk and the Tootsie Roll for me, the support and emotional core for both my parents, seemed gone forever.

D esperate to recapture some of the good feelings we used to have with Nana, or to try to create a diversion from what life had become in her absence, I started planning parties for my family. Birthday parties. Holiday parties. Arbor Day. Any excuse or occasion would do.

A July Fourth weekend loomed, devoid of any plans past watching the fireworks, for which the whole town turned out. Mom needed to rest, but at least she was home. I wanted to celebrate with an Independence Day party. I got her to agree to make both hamburgers and hot dogs—we usually had one or the other—and I walked to the store to buy paper plates, red-white-and-blue napkins, and lots of candy. It was too hot to bake, Mom said, and the bakery was closed for the holiday. So I brought back M&M's and ice cream and Yankee Doodles—chocolate cupcakes with white filling and no icing. They didn't hold a candle to Hostess, but they seemed appropriate to the occasion.

I planned a scaled-down version of a caravan party. We would eat dinner at the kitchen table on the middle level of the house, then go downstairs to the rec room for dessert. I arranged the Yankee Doodles on a plate and poured the candy into dishes, as Mom did for company. I sat down at the dinner table with high hopes. But no one else seemed to realize the party had begun.

After some initial small talk, Dad's gaze fell past us as he lapsed into a distant reverie, chomping silently on his hot dog, his jaw clicking with every bite. Mom's initial effusiveness rapidly subsided into exhausted silence as well. I don't remember what Greg did; to him it was probably just dinner. Which it turned out to be despite my planning and shopping and multilevel choreography.

Afterward, we assembled in the rec room for the requisite network choice of patriotic television movie, *Mr. Smith Goes to Washington*, which none of us wanted to watch. Dad ate a few handfuls of M&M's, Mom and Greg had some ice cream, and the crowd dispersed.

Because it was my party, I was in charge of cleaning it up. Alone in the kitchen, I contemplated the Yankee Doodles. I had thrown away the wrappers and didn't know how else to store them, and by tomorrow it wouldn't even be a holiday anymore. I stood at the counter and crammed one sweet, soft cake after another into my mouth, waiting for liftoff. Surely someone would join me? But all I heard was the sounds of water running in the bathrooms and bedroom doors closing.

The next day Mom said gently, "What a lovely party that was last night," and never questioned the whereabouts of all those Yankee Doodles.

Over the next few years, after more of my parties palled, I gave up. The incessant discussion of the Board of Education gave way to talk of a new house being built somewhere called Scarsdale. The prospect of moving to a famous affluent suburb seemed to lift my parents' spirits, coax them toward happiness. They spoke about it the way they used to talk about Mom's earning her doctorate someday.

I did my best to sustain the more positive mood. There was yet another event at the synagogue, something that was formal and sounded exciting, with hors d'oeuvres and an orchestra, far beyond my meager capabilities at home. I took the savings from my tissue box and bought corsages for Mom, Kiki, and Aunt Marcia. I presented each with an oval cardboard box topped with a plastic lid to showcase . . . what, a gardenia? I still don't know my flowers after all Mom's years in the garden. But they were large and lovely, and each came with a straight pin with a faux-pearl head. The three of them were so pleased and surprised and immediately fastened the corsages on their dresses, exclaiming all the while. They posed for a photo together before they left, their eyes sparkling with pleasure and their cheeks flushed pink. Suddenly, they were girls. And I felt very much a grown-up.

Though I didn't realize it at the time, our family dynamic was indeed changing. Nana's death had unofficially marked the beginning of the rest of my life as Mom's helper. It didn't happen right away or all at once. Some evenings, I would help her grade papers. The tests she gave had two parts, multiple choice and essay, and she would sit me down at the kitchen table with the key of correct multiple choice answers. I would make a check mark or an X after each one, then add up the points. I was very responsible, she said, an enormous help. I assume she had to review my work herself just to be sure, but I felt pretty swell. I needed to feel that way as often as possible, because even though no one had asked my opinion, I wasn't sure I wanted to move to Scarsdale. Passaic was our home, and it had been Nana's home. I relied on my library books more than ever in this period; as they had for Mom and Dad, they provided escape for me.

Mom relied on me more and more to help with Phoebe, and by the time she gave birth to Emmett, when I was thirteen, I was on the job. During those years, my parents could afford a live-in housekeeper—Mom often had evening obligations—so I wasn't exactly Cinderella. But whenever she was teaching or at meetings or generally unavailable, I pitched in. "Do something constructive," she would say. I babysat the younger kids, set the table, packed the lunches. When I was sixteen, my parents bought me a used car. I was delighted until I discovered the reason: I was to drive the carpools for the other three children.

I never questioned these arrangements, any more than it occurred to me to question anything my mother proposed. If she thought it was worth doing, I did it.

Gradually, I became her deputy. Not only had I remained alert, aware, and quick on the uptake, I had added responsible and dependable to my résumé. Phoebe and Emmett put up with my bossing them around because that's the way Mom wanted it. They liked me fine, but they adored her. When Emmett was five or six, he kissed me on the cheek, then shook his head disapprovingly. "Your face is too springy," he said. "Mommy's cheek goes all the way in." It was fine by me if she came first with them. She certainly came first with me. I was never sure who really came first with Mom. Selig maybe, or Dad. Though I always hoped it was me.

As 2005 bled through 2006 into 2007, I often despaired of how I would do if, on any given day, Mom could sit me down at the kitchen table and ask me to tell her what happened that day. I feared my story would be a muddle of anguish, anger, and self-pity.

In search of solace, I opened the folder of recipes she had compiled for me ten years earlier and started to read. Once I took a closer look, I discovered that many of the entries were either incomplete or simply different from what I'd always seen her do. Take the one for fried flounder. Her instructions said to sauté two onions in vegetable oil in order to flavor the oil before frying the fish. I lived in her house for twenty-four years and never once saw her do that. I think Nana did it this way, so maybe she knew she was supposed to but skipped the step and passed it along to me instead.

Whatever the reason, I was faced with the unthinkable: meticulous Mom was proving to be an unreliable narrator. The recklessness of it took my breath away. "Do as I say, not as I do," when applied to a piece of fish, has consequences.

It turned out I wasn't the only one seeking solace in the kitchen and not finding it. Making dinner was the one connection Mom had to her old life, the responsibility that could still anchor her day and give it form. Soon after her surgery, I realized she couldn't remember how to make the simplest of her signature dishes. The instructor of her ceramics class organized a potluck lunch and Mom volunteered to bring her fruit salad. That was something she had made for decades. She would cut up apples, pears, oranges, and bananas, then add a container of defrosted frozen strawberries. It had just enough syrup to bind and sweeten everything in the bowl.

Caroline called to tell me that Mom wasn't sure of the ingredients. It was like saying she didn't know her name. There had never been a recipe; it was just something Mom made as a matter of course. No piece of information in her head seemed safe anymore.

To make things easier, she and Dad started stocking prepared meals from a kosher place nearby. All she had to do was defrost and reheat them. That worked well enough for a while. But the latest combination of antidepressants meant to focus Mom's concentration succeeded only in agitating her. Dad came home from his office early one afternoon, around four o'clock, and found dinner on the table—cold, so it had been there a while.

I tried persuading Mom to let Caroline stay longer each day. She was adamantly opposed. She wanted time to herself. "What do you do in the afternoons?" I asked.

"Nap," she said. "Read. Make dinner."

"Well," I ventured, "you seem anxious about those dinners. Dad says one was already on the table the other day when he came home at four o'clock."

Her silence was injured. "I don't know anything about that," she said.

Goldstein weighed in. If Mom wouldn't accept nine-to-five companionship, then she needed to have structured activities every morning, a place to go, something to look forward to. She needed to socialize, be around other people. The fact that she had never socialized before didn't count, he said; she was going to have to now, whether she liked it or not.

Mom resisted. Women who spent their days sitting around talking or playing games meant one thing to her: Grandma. She had fought against that for the fifty-two years she had worked, and she didn't care what any doctor had to say about it. She wouldn't budge. Goldstein explained that anticipation actually stimulates a chemical in the brain that makes people feel good. It is mentally healthy to have something to look forward to. As he spoke, she listened politely, face frozen, a sure sign of contempt. It seemed eminently clear to her that her days of looking forward had drawn to a close.

That made one of us. I turned to Roberta Epstein for help in tracking down some options in addition to ceramics, the only activity Mom had agreed to. As always, Roberta rose to the occasion. "Absolutely," she trumpeted, her all-purpose exhortation that swept away doubt and marshaled the forces to embrace the day. At least it worked that way on me.

She brought Mom brochures for groups that took trips to museums and Broadway shows, played cards, read books, made paintings. Each activity was more scintillating than the next. She bubbled with enthusiasm, but to no avail. Mom steadfastly refused to be entertained. She wanted to work.

Okay, I said. What if we called a local florist? She still loved flowers. Maybe she could go in for a couple of hours a day. Roberta checked it out. Not possible, she discovered. There were issues about insurance, about being responsible in the workplace for someone who might not be responsible for herself.

What about Iona? I asked Mom. She had worked there for thirty-five years, she knew the people, loved the place. Everything was familiar. I could call someone in the psychology department to see if we could figure out something part-time, maybe even in the library. When I proposed this, we were sitting alone at the dining room table having tea. As she had with Roberta's suggestions, she immediately rejected it.

I pushed. Why not? She looked down at her hands. When she looked up she struggled against crying. "I've lost my confidence," she said, her voice breaking. "I can't."

I could understand that. It was her anger—deep, epic anger—at her situation, at the doctors, at the very notion of cooperation that unnerved me. Yes, she had plenty to be angry about. But what about the power of positive thinking she had always forced on me? Or even the basic survival instinct to adapt? "No" and "I can't remember" were her stock responses. To placate me, she would appear to cooperate, though Goldstein wasn't fooled. "It's easier for her to say 'I can't remember' than actually try to remember," he said.

When we went to see him together, he would ask her questions. "Which female senator would most likely run for president?" "What's the name of the park nearest your house?" She couldn't answer. Ten minutes later, when he asked again, she knew everything she needed to know about Hillary Clinton. Had she blown him off the first time? He thought so. I was unconvinced. Her polio and lifelong hatred of doctors was ancient history by now, wasn't it? There had to be some statute of limitations—acting like a three-year-old in your seventies wasn't just reckless, it was dangerous. As far as I could see, her life depended on getting the answers right.

Over time it seemed that Goldstein and I were both correct. Sometimes she simply didn't want to be bothered. Sometimes she genuinely didn't remember. But more and more, her brain was short-circuiting. One minute she was with us, the next, not. That was the basis for her anger, her loss of confidence, and her withdrawal. I thought of the days after the bypass surgery when she would call to say, "I feel like myself again," her voice ringing with determination, as if it were an act of will. What a relief it must have been to her to believe that, for however long the feeling lasted. What terror she must have experienced as her core, her very essence, flickered on and off and back again, each time not quite as brightly.

I called a friend who was involved with a senior center. She referred me to the man in charge, who could not have been lovelier. They'd be happy to have Mom work as a volunteer. Mom resisted. I begged her to try it, and Caroline promised to stay with her the entire time. Finally she relented and off they went. Caroline called later that afternoon. Mom was fine during the morning activities, she said. Someone came in and spoke, then there was dancing—she actually danced with one of the older gentlemen—then lunch was served. When Mom finished eating, Caroline told her she needed to clear the dishes and cutlery on all the tables. Mom folded her arms. "I'll clean my own place, that's all," she said. "Why should I clean up after everyone else?" The next day, she refused to go back. I called the lovely man and bid him farewell.

At the Jewish Community Center where Mom took the ceramics class, Roberta and I found a twice-a-month lecture series. The array of speakers was interesting, and we figured that anything resembling a class couldn't be a bad idea. Mom seemed to like it. But when I met her back at her apartment twenty minutes after a lecture ended, she could not remember the day's topic. Caroline would dutifully relay the finer points of how Torah scrolls were made, dropping broad hints each step of the way to jog her memory, to no avail.

We were due back to Weinberger for a repeat of the Doppler test. As Mom and I waited near a nurses' station at Mount Sinai, we tried to ignore the bed that someone had parked a few yards away. An elderly woman lay on her side, drifting in and out of consciousness.

Mom turned to face me. "I want you to kill me," she said solemnly. For decades, she had insisted that if she was mentally compromised in any way, her children were to pull the plug. But the scenarios we'd imagined never included her being compromised outside a hospital, lasting years on end.

"I can't kill you," I answered steadily. "I have a husband and two stepsons and a job and a mortgage. Someone will find out and then I'll have to go to prison."

She sighed, exasperated.

"I know this issue has always been important to you," I said. "So if you feel strongly about it, I understand that. You can end your own life. There are plenty of places that can help you do that."

She was monumentally offended. "Committing suicide is against the Jewish religion!" she declared.

I was dumbfounded. "So is committing murder! Did you ever think of that?"

Apparently not.

Our move to Scarsdale, when I was twelve, ushered in an especially dark period for my family. The house was red brick with shiny black shutters. It stood stark and apart, all sharp edges, near the end of the block on a cul-de-sac. A few small bushes were planted in front, but not enough. Inside, the new-house smell was overpowering, and whatever furniture we brought with us looked as misplaced as we felt. Mom kept changing the layout of the den, tossing and turning each piece into different combinations until Dad fell over an oddly positioned chair. He made her stop.

The wish to go back to Passaic loomed large. Mom was no longer the toast of the town. She was stocking up on sheets and towels and looking for a job. Dad had gone from being a hometown boy, knowing everyone and everything, to being an outsider, and an outsider toward the bottom of the local economic scale at that. The really rich people lived on the other side of town, in the grander, older houses nestled into lush lawns, buffered by oak and willow trees—not naked on their lots, like our house and those surrounding it. At night, when we were supposed to be sleeping, we would hear strange noises. The house is settling, our parents told us. It sounded like bones breaking.

Dad's schedule had always been regular; he came home from work each night in time to sit down to dinner at six o'clock sharp. After the news, he would go straight to bed. He lay there reading and listening to the radio and watching television, all at once, while the rest of the family was downstairs. During the winter, he would make a fire in the den fireplace before retreating upstairs. On weekends, he took naps. He hated going on vacation and did so only when Mom insisted she needed the ocean. For years, for a week or two each summer, they rented an apartment in Amagansett, where he counted the days until he could go home. For all Mom's love of the sun, she wasn't essentially much different. During my high school years, she got Dad to take us to the Caribbean for a week each Christmas, although once we were back, all she did was fold the laundry, wash the dishes, and repeat how good it was to be home, like a prayer.

So, in the early days of the Scarsdale house, everyone was feeling especially fragile. My own entrée into seventh-grade society had not gone swimmingly. I went to school wearing a jumper and kneesocks. The other girls wore miniskirts and stockings. And shaved their legs, which I was not yet allowed to do. My hair was short, their hair was long. I brought lunches packed by Mom, salami or leftover hamburger or something else reeking of garlic and horseradish mustard that you could smell by ten o'clock in the middle of math class. She used whatever paper bag she had lying around. The other girls' mothers picked up their daughters' sandwiches at the local deli. They were neat and trim and filled with odor-free turkey and lettuce, gift-wrapped in white paper and tucked inside a crisp brown bag. The other girls all skied and played paddle tennis. I had never done either. Academically, I was wrestling with the transition from overcrowded urban public school to top-tier suburban school, and I found myself behind in every subject.

One evening, I was sitting at the kitchen table after dinner, trying to do my homework. The boiler hadn't kicked in and the air was chilly. Math was a horror show of its own. I couldn't make heads or tails of it. Neither, that night, could Mom. She summoned Dad.

At first, I thought this was a fine idea. But I soon realized that Dad's brain was as ill-suited to the new math as mine was, and he had far less patience than Mom. It took a very few minutes for the situation to go from bad to worse, with him going about it all wrong and me trying to correct him by explaining what the teacher had said while he kept telling me to shut up and Mom lit yet another cigarette at her end of the table.

Finally, I could bear it no longer. I stood, throwing my hands up in a grand gesture of disgust, and said, "Forget it!" In a flash, so fast that I never saw it coming, as they say—and they are right—Dad drew back and punched me flat on the nose. Screams ensued and blood spurted everywhere—on the table, on the floor. I ran toward the staircase, with Mom right behind me. "Hold your hands up," she yelled. "Don't get blood on the carpet! It's brand-new!"

Upstairs in the bathroom, I leaned my head back as she provided tissues, then a washcloth. When I was no longer a threat to the carpeting, she allowed me to go back to my room. I lay in bed, head still tilted back, feeling as low as I ever had. A new house, a new school, not nearly enough friends, and now this. Not to mention that I hadn't come close to finishing my homework.

Mom came in. Ah. She was going to comfort me, reassure me.

"You owe your father an apology," she said.

I waited for her to explain what she possibly could mean, but she remained silent. "I do?" I asked finally. "He hit *me*."

"Yes, but he said he hit you because you raised your hands to him. So he was defending himself."

After all my years at the library, I knew that as plotlines went, this one was barely believable. I had not raised my hands to him, I had thrown my hands up in frustration. I knew from my reading that this was an option—in books, people threw their hands up all the time. Though wringing their hands was something else entirely. I never could figure out what it meant. I'm still not sure I've ever seen it.

"I didn't raise my hands to him, I was getting up to leave the table! I was frustrated!"

She was unmoved. "You have to apologize." Her face was grim, haggard—a shadow of herself, the books would say. I could see she knew his version was a lie. So why was she selling me out? It wasn't the first time, and it would not be the last. My relationship with her, which was so special, was apparently not special enough to withstand the demands of her husband. To say that I intended to attack him physically was a lie. The rules about lying applied to me and me only, it seemed.

She waited silently until I went into their bedroom to apologize for something I hadn't done. Dad was lying in bed reading. He barely looked up. "Hmmm-hmmm," he intoned, as if to imply that he couldn't care less. Insult to injury, the books would say.

But after this sorry episode, Mom quietly won me back. I don't remember how, but she did it. I loved her and I trusted her, even though she had betrayed me. I wanted to believe that this experience was an aberration, the exception, but I knew it was not. I saw that she could not voice her opposition to my father; that would be my job. I could stand up and say no. I was stronger than she was. I had known it when the car pulled back into the driveway of the dark house on Terhune Avenue the night we were supposed to have run away to the hotel filled with women in ball gowns. I knew it then and I knew it now.

As best she could, she continued to support me, listening and encouraging. When I wrote a paper in my eighth-grade English class on *Johnny Tremain* and didn't get an A, Dad took it in hand one night at dinner. He made a show of clearing his throat before reading sentences mockingly out loud to illustrate how inept they were—and with his job writing press releases and annual reports for corporations, he knew everything about writing. Mom found me in my bed afterward and dried my tears. She assured me that my ideas were smart, that with practice I would get the hang of writing eventually. She even told me I was pretty, though I was clearly stalled at what she called an "awkward" age, and looked more than anything like an unbaked muffin.

We soldiered on this way for years. When Dad yelled at her, I leapt to her defense. She let me. I had gone from being helper to lawyer, bodyguard, and godfather. During the ensuing melee—there was usually a melee—where was Mom, whose honor I was defending? Vanished. Afterward, she admonished me that Dad deserved my empathy and understanding. He had had a grueling experience with his own father. It wasn't his fault.

Did that mean it was *mine*? She switched tactics. "I know you are angry at your father," she said. "I understand that. But that can be a positive force. Anger is a great motivator."

It never occurred to me to butt out. As her child, I adored her blindly and forgave her every time. I could protect myself. I think it was simpler, quite often, for her to love me than it was for her to love him.

The feeling of fracture in our family persisted. Maybe it would have been easier on everyone if we had stayed closer to Passaic. Much of the social life in Scarsdale centered on country clubs where families played tennis or golf, swam in the summers, ate dinner on the weekends. We did not belong to a country club. They were too expensive, not to mention concertedly frivolous— people playing games who might just as well have read a book. Unabridged. And the cliquishness at their base offended both my parents.

Mom found her job at Iona, but that made her the same outcast among women in Scarsdale that she had once been in Passaic. Dad found a new synagogue and a couple of new pals, and he and Mom became friendly with a neighboring family or two. But mostly, they kept to themselves.

The summer I was fourteen got off to a calamitous start. Greg and Dad had been setting up the barbecue on the deck of our house on Memorial Day, and Dad used what he thought was lighter fluid to ignite it. The unmarked can was actually gasoline, and it exploded in his hand. He was severely burned and spent five months in intensive care, undergoing skin grafts and reconstructive surgery on his hand. Greg was hurt somewhat less seriously, but he, too, spent months in the hospital, recovering.

Grandma and her husband came to live at our house to help with Phoebe and Emmett so that Mom could be at the hospital, and I went off to sleepaway camp as usual at the end of June. Mom missed the regular parents' visiting day, but she came another time, and we sat together under a big tree near the main entrance. She talked about Dad and Greg, the experience of going back and forth between them. She told me about coming home late one night and washing her face in her bathroom. It had been a particularly hellish day, and she began to rage at God about allowing her husband and child to be in such grievous pain. "I lifted my hands up," she told me, her face flushing, "and I was yelling at God, 'How can you do this to my family?' And I meant to say, 'God, I hate you!' But instead, I said, 'God, I love you.' And I started to cry."

I wasn't quite sure what this meant, whether she had spoken to God or He had spoken to her, but I found it deeply disturbing. I wished that instead of us sitting under this tree alone on the wrong day, with my disappointing last-quarter report card open between us and a lone corned beef sandwich, we'd been together on the regular visiting day, with Dad stretching out on my cot to take a nap, bony knees facing skyward, while Mom unpacked every little thing my heart desired from home.

But here she was, talking about railing at God, her crimson face looking resolute yet abstracted, as if she were still listening for something and maybe even hearing it. I couldn't understand it and I have never forgotten it. She was in some sort of mano a mano confrontation with God and his minions that was as muscular as it was spiritual, as solitary as synagogue was communal. The docile Mom lighting candles on Friday nights, covering her face with her hands and praying for her family, kissing us sweetly, each in turn, when she had finished, was nowhere in evidence. The gentle Mom who ministered after a confrontation with Dad, quiet and soothing, was gone. This Mom was primal and raw and powerful—engulfed in flames of her own.

B ack at Terhune Avenue, Mom used to make a dish called Chicken Polynesian. This was a skillet concoction that featured canned cling peaches in heavy syrup and green peppers. I can smell it as vividly as if she made it yesterday, savory and sweet and beautiful, the peppers emerald against the golden chicken and peaches. To me, one of the glimmering achievements of housewifery in the age of Betty Crocker was exactly this: transporting your family to a foreign land with the help of Del Monte. It seemed the ideal way to travel—within the safety of your own home.

Of course, what I considered exotic as a child is laughable now. Go online and you can find an actual Polynesian to come to your door and make the chicken for you. Through the years, my culinary travel fantasies expanded to include time travel, for the ultimate caravan dinner party. Although when I think of all the stops I want to make, I can't contain it in one meal. It has to be a buffet.

First, I try Nana's lentil soup. Finally! Everyone always raved about it, but I refused to ever eat it because I thought it looked like mud. Then I fill a plate with the tiny meatballs she used to put in her chicken fricassee with the brown sauce—no gizzards or flabby wings in sight. I have the latkes, of course, and the kreplach, dipped in applesauce. Then Mom's baby lamb chops, covered in Lawry's and garlic powder and broiled to a crisp. I follow those with her frankfurter goulash. This is cut-up frankfurters cooked with onion, stewed tomatoes, and green peppers, served on top of white rice, dotted with French's mustard. It's the ultimate addiction: deli meat sauce. Then there's Aunt Marcia's cauliflower, mashed, with salt and pepper and bread crumbs. And I marvel at the unfettered decadence of Mom's bronzed cheese blintzes, fried in butter and heaped with sour cream.

Oh! But now I think I have to start all over again because I didn't even see the platter of Smoky Joes. There they are, next to the Sloppy Joes, which are not loose hamburger in buns, but triple-decker sandwiches of pastrami, corned beef, and tongue on rye with coleslaw, Russian dressing, and mustard. These are from Lipson's, our long-gone deli, every piece a perfect triangle, without the crusts. The Smoky Joes are from Karpen's, our appetizing store in Passaic. These are the same idea: rye or marbled rye, layered with kippered salmon salad, coleslaw, Swiss cheese, Muenster cheese, lox, and cream cheese spread. Salty, smooth, slight crunch from the coleslaw. All mine.

I try to find some room for the disappeared Entenmann's Brownie Crumb Ring. Misleadingly named, this was golden cake with mocha frosting and crumbles of brownies on top. I don't bother with a plate. I never did. I cut it and eat it in hunks, from the box.

Then I sit back with Nana, she with her glass of tea and cube of sugar, and Mom, who has her Dewar's on the rocks with a splash of soda and a twist of lemon in hand, her downfall sliced on a platter before her. Grandma stops in for a caramel sundae, and I give her the highlights of all the episodes of *Ryan's Hope* that she missed.

I am full.

Frankfurter Goulash

8–10 Hebrew National frankfurters
3 tablespoons canola oil
2 medium onions, diced
2 (14½-ounce) cans Del Monte stewed tomatoes
1 (8-ounce) can Del Monte tomato sauce
1 large green pepper, cut into strips, then crosswise
   into thirds
White rice and French's or deli mustard, for serving

In a medium saucepan, bring five cups of water to a boil. Add franks and simmer 8 to 10 minutes. Drain and set aside.

Heat the oil in a large skillet and add the onions. Cook over medium heat until soft, 8 to 10 minutes. Drain one can of the stewed tomatoes and add to pan; add the second can with the juice, then break up the tomatoes with a wooden spoon. Cook over medium heat for 5 to 10 minutes to thicken the sauce, then add the canned tomato sauce and green peppers and simmer for 10 minutes longer.

Cut the franks into bite-sized pieces and add to pan, stirring well. Cover and let simmer on low heat for 10 minutes.

Serve with white rice. To eat, mix the goulash with the rice and dot the franks with French's or deli mustard.

Serves 4

Five

· ● · · · · ·

As I got older, my friendship with my mother thrived. We'd watch TV together every night in the den while Dad stayed upstairs as usual with a book, the radio, and his own TV. Mom and I went to the movies, hunted for bargains at Loehmann's. My friend Sandy, who was Mormon, used to hang out with us. She'd come for coffee in the morning and cocktails in the evening. She loved Mom. All my friends did. When one of them thought she was pregnant and was afraid to tell her own mother, Mom brought her to Planned Parenthood and waited while she got a pregnancy test. When it was negative, Mom gave her a personal symposium on birth control.

Time did not seem to improve my relationship with my father, however. On college vacations, my girlfriends from high school would all make dates to meet their commuting fathers in the city for lunch. I proposed to Dad that we do the same and he agreed. The night before, he, Mom, and I had our customary row before I left to go out with friends. The next morning, I got dressed and put on my makeup before heading downstairs. On the kitchen table, I found a note. *Girls with big mouths don't get lunch dates*, it read. Over that summer, I don't think he spoke one word to me. If I said "Good morning," he didn't respond. If I asked a question, he didn't answer. If I walked into a room, he didn't look up. It was exactly how he treated Grandma.

Looking back, I wonder why I didn't walk out the front door to go to college and keep on going, abdicating my role in this pernicious cycle. But I couldn't do it. When Mom was good to me, I basked in her love. When she sold me out, I wasn't angry with her, I was angry at Dad. He made it so easy.

In the meantime, Phoebe and Emmett had replaced me and Greg in the household. Phoebe was beautiful in the same effortlessly preordained way that Mom and Grandma were. As a child, she was funny and sweet, delightful company. She idolized me and I liked it. It seemed inevitable that as Phoebe got older, she would join our merry band.

But the bond that Mom and I forged often excluded her. And Mom's "Tell me everything that happened today" didn't have the same effect on Phoebe that it had on me. Phoebe noticed plenty of things in the course of a day, but she didn't leap to attention in order to describe them. She didn't like being grilled. She didn't want to be better than me or as good as Mom. She wanted to know why she didn't have a mother who stayed home like all the other mothers. She didn't like that a neighbor had to pick her up from school when she was sick because Mom was teaching and couldn't do it herself. When she was in grade school, she used to stand on her desk and scream. She was more mutiny than deputy.

Unfortunately for Phoebe, she was, in Mom's eyes, very much like Grandma. She was a shopper, not a reader. She loved to socialize and had a talent for making—and keeping—reams of friends. She felt free to invite them to our house without notice and offer sleepovers and dinners without checking with Mom. She was both eager to please and glad to break rules; one day when Mom was at work, Phoebe persuaded a neighbor to come over and paint her bedroom walls bright blue with the word "Phoebe" on one wall in big purple letters. Mom was apoplectic. The two of them had fights of the sort I had with Dad, though theirs were interspersed with prolonged periods of kissing, cuddling, and blessed peace.

Dad much preferred Phoebe to me. When he saw me reading a book all day every day, he used to say kiddingly, "Girls who read are dangerous." Phoebe wasn't dangerous. She didn't love books, she loved babies. Even when she was only six or seven, she'd seek them out at the pool during the summer. When Mom spouted Grandma's big-picture philosophy of life, Marriage and Children, Phoebe was on board. I talked a good game, but I was more ambivalent. Being a child was not fun for me. Being parents was plainly not fun for my parents, though Mom had her moments with each of us, certainly. I was in no rush to decide, one way or the other. Once when I was home from college, Mom handed me a poem by Judith Viorst and watched me read it. "Good," she said when she was confident I had teared up. "I just wanted to make sure you had a maternal instinct."

I planned accordingly. Chernobyl happened right when I was scheduled to leave for a trip to Russia. My gynecologist advised me not to go; there was so much radiation, I might never get pregnant. I stayed home.

Even so, when I saw toddlers in strollers on the street, I would automatically think, *No, thanks,* or *Not yet.* I had none of the baby hunger Phoebe and Mom shared. Phoebe was an avid babysitter, a job I found tedious at best. Mom would approach random women holding babies in the bank or supermarket and ask to cop a feel—squeezing the plump leg of a mystified child just made her day.

The only thing that happened next was I got older and older without getting married. There were a few reasons for this. The first, which was odd for someone so committed to having a career, was I couldn't find one I liked. (I could never marry until I knew what my own life would be.) I had remained terrible at math, so business was out of the question. I had none of Mom's aptitude for science. I couldn't be a writer; Dad had made that clear. My college guidance counselors thought law school wasn't a bad idea; with that training you could do anything. I had my doubts—I worked for a few weeks as a legal proofreader and thought I might die of boredom—but I enrolled in a class to prepare for the law boards. And never went. The night before the test, for which I had studied maybe fifteen minutes, I looked again at a sample and couldn't figure out the questions, let alone the answers. I tearfully told Mom I couldn't go through with it. She was supportive; there were plenty of jobs under the sun.

And so there were, but first there was the Bread Loaf Writers'

Conference. This was an annual event at Middlebury College in Vermont, and my writing professor had encouraged me to apply for the summer before my senior year. I was accepted as a participant, which meant I didn't just listen to the great writers of the day read from their own work; they would read mine, too, and advise me. This was an exciting prospect, since *The World According to Garp* was all the rage that summer and John Irving was one of the advisers. And so cute.

When I arrived in August, fresh from my law boards meltdown, I discovered that my adviser would be the novelist Stanley Elkin. Not cute at all. Middle-aged, with a gray complexion and sour expression, understandably enraged at having to suffer the indignities of multiple sclerosis. One night outside someone else's reading, he and his wife had a very loud, very public fight. Our meeting kept being postponed.

On the morning when we finally sat down together, he pulled out my stories and dropped them on the table. "So where do you go to school?" he asked.

"Wheaton College," I said. He looked blank.

"It's a small women's college in Massachusetts."

He smirked. "For small women?"

That was the nice part. Not since the excoriation of *Johnny Tremain* had I encountered such vitriol. When he was done, I must have looked as devastated as I felt. He didn't soften, but he did offer a crumb: You write short, clear sentences, he said. You'd probably do well in journalism.

Coming from a famous novelist, there wasn't a more condescending thing to say to the likes of me. And the truth was, I was something of a washout when it came to serious literary aspirations. I cared just as much about Judith Krantz as I did Jane Austen. I packed up and left the conference early. There didn't seem to be much point in hanging around.

With the option of law school eliminated, I turned my focus to graduate school. Certainly not in writing. After Bread Loaf, I could barely write my name. Instead, I spent three years earning a Master of Fine Arts in theater administration at the Yale School of Drama and went to work for the Shubert Organization, the largest theater owners on Broadway. I loved drama school. I loved the theater. But I did not love being a house manager. You went to work at seven p.m., listened to customers complain about their seats, listened to more complaints about the line for the ladies' room at intermission, collected three lost umbrellas when the show ended, and went home at eleven. On matinee days you got to do it twice.

The good news was that most days were free for job hunting. But what was I hunting for? I had no idea. Mom had focused on her doctorate so she could teach. To me, teaching had the same allure as babysitting. If a student didn't understand it in thirty seconds, I had no doubt I would scold, "Quick on the uptake! Alert! Pay attention!" I hired a career counselor, who sent me on 165 informational interviews, many of them in advertising. I almost became a junior account executive before realizing I was about to make my life's work Prell shampoo.

Mom continued to be sympathetic, for the most part. Although, at this point, she did suggest I marry my longtime boyfriend, "just so you can have the experience of marriage." Never mind that he wasn't Jewish and she didn't like him as much as his mother didn't like me. She had taken to saving housewares catalogs for me, flagging pages featuring place settings for twelve. This wasn't quite as irritating as it sounds. My parents had both fought a lifelong struggle to feel normal, to look like everyone else, when neither ever did. Buying cups and saucers looked like everyone else. Maybe once they owned them, they would feel embraced somehow. It hadn't quite worked out that way for them, but Mom held out hope for me. Maybe if I had the dishes, the rest would come.

Still, she bore with me as I continued on my informational interviews and combed through the Help Wanted section of *The New York Times*. The employment agencies I went to advised me to throw out my résumé. A master's degree from Yale combined with no typing or shorthand skills was not a winning strategy. I was overqualified and underqualified at the same time. One agency had a listing for a job at a start-up magazine that turned out to be *Elle*. For years, I'd stumbled through *Elle* in my half-baked high school French at the hair salon. Now, after Bloomingdale's included the magazine in a promotion on France, Rupert Murdoch figured out that Americans would buy it if they could read it, so he was starting an English-language edition in the United States.

The editor in chief was a genteel blonde who came from fashion and had never run a major magazine before. My extreme lack of secretarial skills didn't seem to bother her. I could learn the business from the ground up, she said. I might become an editor someday, or maybe a writer. For real? I was ecstatic. What could be better than entering a profession based on Mom's mantra, "the whole truth and nothing but," combined with the dubious talent she called "sticking your nose where it doesn't belong"?

On my first day, there was a big meeting. I was asked to get coffee for three different people, and when they were all assembled in the editor's office, the door closed with me on the outside. Learning the business from the ground up was apparently a less direct process than I had envisioned. By lunchtime, I was crying in the ladies' room. I soon discovered that I wasn't the only one. The editor in chief was crying, too. Whenever Mr. Murdoch called to speak to her, she would instruct me to tell him she was "in the market." That was supposed to mean she was out and about, somewhere in the fashion world, but she was really in her office with the door closed, overwhelmed and sobbing. Obviously, this situation could not last. The premier issue was to bow in September, it was already June, and the place was a shambles. Barely three months after I was hired, my boss was fired.

A crew of Murdoch executives, all men, descended on the office. "Take a letter," one snapped at me, starting to dictate. I wrote as quickly as I could, but he stopped me. "No shorthand?" he asked. I shook my head no. He sighed, long and hard. Those lost umbrellas flashed before my eyes.

Enter Eve Pollard.

Eve had been a newspaper and magazine editor on Fleet Street and she was, in short, a force of nature. With her frosted blond hair and violet lipstick, she was canny and game and as fresh at the end of a fifteen-hour day as she was at the start. She had enormous breasts, and on the initial Saturday she commanded all hands on deck, she made her entrance in a sleeveless black T-shirt that said MUSCLE across her chest.

On her first official day in the office, she sat me down and listened to my woebegone job history. "Right," she said briskly when I'd finished, and then she made a deal with me. She expected to stay in the job for six to eight months, get the magazine up and running, then return to London. During that time, she assured me, she would work me into the ground while asking me to do every distasteful thing I could imagine, from picking up her dry cleaning to babysitting her son. In return, in every single issue she promised to run an article I wrote, so that by the time she left, I would have a portfolio to show the new editor and would be eligible for a promotion. I practically wept with gratitude.

Good to her word, Eve frayed my nerves daily. The restaurant Montrachet had just opened in Tribeca, and she wanted to take Calvin Klein there for lunch. "Book a table for one o'clock Friday," she instructed.

I must have called fifty times. "Sorry," I told her. "I can't get through."

She looked at me uncomprehendingly. Then, in the very calm voice she used instead of yelling, she said, "Go down there and book it in person." As a journalist, she knew that sometimes the best way was to just show up.

I learned very quickly how to get things done, without explanations or excuses. My lack of shorthand aside, I became a good secretary, and gradually a good reporter. The woman simply refused to take no for an answer. If someone did say no, it was my job to find out why, and figure out how to make him or her say yes. That was the part she wanted to hear. How I got there concerned her not at all.

Eve's counterpart was a Frenchman named Regis (pronounced ray-ZHEECE) Pagniez. If she was the words, he was the music—or, more accurately, the visuals. He was talented and smart and very good at pretending that his English was terrible whenever someone said something he didn't want to hear. He would walk into the art department draped in models, who would spot themselves on the wall and squeal in delight. *"C'est moi! C'est moi! C'est moi!"*

The staff very quickly learned to play Mommy off Daddy, and here I was in my element. Protect Mom? I was a pro at that! You need to see Eve? Why? When? For how long? Regis said *what?*

When I wasn't being a cop, I had something of a ball. The girl who ran the accessories closet was a good egg who loaned us jewelry from the photo shoots to wear out on dates. Items were lost, broken, forgotten. She was soon gone and I missed her mightily. This was in the mid-1980s, and while we all had computers, no one really knew how to use them. On days an issue was to close, dinner was ordered in and the staff supplied the booze and we sat around until midnight, waiting for layouts. We joked about making up T-shirts: ELLE MAGAZINE. WE NEVER CLOSE.

As for my writing, Eve kept her promise. The magazine had a section called "Faces," which were very short profiles, about five hundred words. My first assignment was Bernadette Peters, who would be starring on Broadway in Andrew Lloyd Webber's *Song and Dance* the month after *Elle* debuted. She was at the Williamstown Theatre Festival rehearsing it over the summer, but there was no time for me to go to the Berkshires to and see her; I'd have to interview her by phone.

I went to the Performing Arts Library at Lincoln Center and spent a full Saturday reading every last word ever written about Bernadette Peters. I made lists and lists of questions. The only person who knew more about her was her mother. It turned out the only time Peters could speak to me was in the evening, after a performance. I sat on my futon in my apartment on Bank Street, heart pounding as I dialed the number. My hand was so sweaty, the pen kept slipping. In my other hand, I clutched my teddy bear. When she came on the line, she sounded very tired, but she was perfectly nice and answered every question. I wrote it up, read it three times to my friend Philip, and brought it in.

Eve's husband, Nick Lloyd, who also worked for Murdoch then and was one of the executives calling the shots, asked me for my piece. I watched him read it as he walked into the empty office next to Eve's. He stood there, still reading, his back to me, and I knew immediately it was no good.

He came back to my desk. "You've never done this before." It was more statement than question. I nodded. He brought over two other articles. "Like this," he said. I read them. Of course. These were conversational. Mine was a term paper. I rewrote it. Eve ran it, under the headline "Song and Dance Ma'am." God bless her.

By the time she left, I had the six pieces in my portfolio that she had promised. I agreed to spend a few months easing the transition for the woman who replaced her, who was no fun at all, though quite the entrepreneur. Every day after lunch, she would drop a slip of paper on my desk, on which she'd written *Coat check $1*, for me to include on her expense reports. Two weeks' vacation and summers excluded, she made an extra $210 a year, whether she wore a coat or not.

Soon enough, I was promoted to assistant features editor. I wrote captions and headlines and spoke to movie publicists no one else wanted to speak to. And kept writing real pieces every month, a privilege that was never revoked. In a business filled with mean girls, Eve had been both fair and generous to me. It was a big deal then and it's a big deal now.

When I left *Elle* for *Mirabella* three years later, I was the entertainment editor, and I'd been recruited by the editor Adam Moss to write a column called "Inside Theater" for *7 Days*, a competing weekly to *New York* magazine. The column ran only twice a month, so I could easily do it in addition to fulfilling my editing duties at *Mirabella*. Suddenly, the years I had spent collecting those lost umbrellas came in handy; I had industry sources high and low, all happy to chat.

In the meantime, the longtime boyfriend and I had split. We'd been invited to a corporate reception one night to celebrate the opening of a Rodin exhibit at the Metropolitan Museum of Art, but he called that afternoon to say he had to leave town unexpectedly to see clients in Texas. I went alone. In that relationship, I was used to doing almost everything alone, very much the way my parents operated. At the exhibit I may have been the only one paying attention to the art; I was so absorbed that it took me a while to notice another woman circling me. Finally, she introduced herself. She told me she was engaged—to my boyfriend. It turned out he had an additional fiancée, as well. Suffice it to say this was all news to me.

How could such a thing have happened? I spent countless hours deconstructing it. The truth was, over ten years he and I had grown further and further apart, but were too immature to admit that. And let's face it, my role models for intimacy were not exactly textbook. Having a boyfriend who felt free to behave this badly said as much about me as it did about him. Phoebe used to tease me, when we were younger, that I'd missed sharing in nursery school—not because I was stingy, but because I was so rigidly self-contained. Every stone, pebble, grain of sand, had to be sorted, scheduled, and accounted for. There was no room for error. Or company. Except on a very limited basis. Mom used to scorn the husbands of women who showed up at the beauty salon or went shopping with them. "Enough already! Go away!" she would say derisively.

The truth was, when it came to intimacy, Mom and I had the semblance of a marriage going ourselves. We planned outings small and large—to the museum, the ballet, Pizza & Brew. Standing side by side with her over the sale table of cashmere sweaters at

Bonwit Teller on the Friday each year after Thanksgiving, I was exhilarated by the sense of limitless possibility and great fun—both hallmarks of a winning relationship. Of course, I should have cut loose the absentee boyfriend long before, but I liked sex, hated the idea of dating, and romanticized the sentimental conceit of marrying a childhood sweetheart; it seemed like its own kind of family to me.

But here I was, dating again, and none too happy about it. I preferred working, especially writing and reporting the theater column. My job at *Mirabella* was more regimented than it was at *Elle*, and my writing there wasn't always what Grace Mirabella—Miss Mirabella, she wanted to be called—had in mind. Much of the staff followed her from *Vogue*, and I turned out to be a misfit among this cache of joyless creatures who were dancing a daily minuet of power and intimidation that I couldn't seem to learn and couldn't bring myself to care about. One editor actually stood at the reception desk in the morning, clocking how many minutes past nine a.m. an employee arrived. The tardiest employee was usually me. One day, I was handed a portrait of Lauren Hutton and told to write a substantial caption. This being years before Botox, I made mention of the creases and wrinkles on her face (I thought they looked cool, not realizing I was meant to ignore them). Miss M. tossed the caption, and it seemed she might toss me, too.

When the arts editor of *7 Days* left, I applied for the job and got it. Ten weeks later when the magazine folded, I was unprepared and alarmed. I had never been out of work before. Luckily,

The New York Times, ever on the lookout for a sale, scooped up me, Adam Moss, and a handful of other writers and editors. I became a reporter in the culture department and, in addition, started writing the theater column.

Eve was thrilled for me. She called one day from London. "Hello, darling," she began. That did not bode well; she needed a favor. "Do you think you can run up to Bloomie's and pick up some pints of pads?" she asked. She meant the shoulder pads they used to sell in the late eighties and early nineties, packed in what looked like ice cream containers.

I started to panic. It would also mean a trip to the post office. "Eve, I can't. I'm on deadline. My piece is due in an hour and I'm smack in the middle."

"Oh, but you have a whole hour," she wheedled. "You can be up and back in no time."

I looked over at my editor, glaring at his computer screen as the department clock ticked. What was I thinking? I said no to her, for the first time. Our relationship survived.

During the years that I wrote for *7 Days*, one of the hottest topics in the theater world was the *Times* theater critic, also known as the Butcher of Broadway, Frank Rich. I had met him by accident during my first few months at *Elle*. A theater producer invited me to the opening night of a play called *Doubles*, and we skipped the party to find a copy of the review. My date knew about a newsstand in the East Fifties that got the papers early. When we arrived, we found the *Times* critic, also waiting. The two men knew each other, and the three of us began to talk. Frank had had a fight with the copy desk, he said. There was some nudity in the play, and he had written the word "penis" in his review—a word that had never been used in the paper, at that point, outside Science Times. The editors forbade it. Frank got mad and left. But once he'd cooled down, he was curious to see what had happened, so he walked out to get a copy.

The three of us stood there talking for two more hours. *What a nice guy,* I thought. Not a butcher or a monster at all. He was married, had two small sons. When the paper finally came, he bent it open the way men do, not caring how black their hands turn. He held it up to the streetlight. History was made; "penis" had been published in the arts section. When we all said good night, he held out the paper to me. "Do you want it?" he asked. "Sure," I said. As I rode home in a cab, I remember thinking that I would have this to show my grandkids one day. As a matter of fact, I still do.

Two years passed. I heard Frank and his wife had split. I pondered that notion for a few days. I had found him to be a completely likable person, not to mention smart, smart, smart, and very funny. Maybe this was the moment to ask for some writing tips. (Lame, yes, but it was all I had.) I called the *Times* and left a message with his assistant, mentioning I had met him on a street corner with my date two years earlier. He called back in fifteen minutes. He remembered.

I wish I could say we lived happily ever after from that moment forward, but he had married young and was intent on making up for lost time. We became friends, then friends with benefits, as they say. In the aftermath of my serial fiancé, I was none too keen myself to leap into anything serious, though with my advancing age, nothing would have made Mom happier. Every Sunday night she'd call me. Where had I been that weekend? Who had I seen? Did I meet anyone? Yes, Izzy Twersky, I snapped. "These conversations are officially over," I finally informed her. "My private life is mine and it is not open for discussion. If I meet anyone or have anything to tell you, I'll make sure to let you know. Otherwise, my personal life is off-limits."

That got her attention. She wasn't used to anything being off-limits regarding me.

Before invoking radio silence, though, I did tell her about going to dinner one night with Frank. We were in a steakhouse, the kind of place that, in those days, made Caesar salads from scratch—but only for two or more. I told her Frank wanted to order one, but I'd said no.

She could hardly believe her ears. "What's wrong with Caesar salad?" she asked sharply.

"Well, raw eggs, for starters," I said. "They're slimy. Anchovies are gross, too, and Parmesan smells bad."

The silence was deafening for at least five seconds before she burst out, *"Just eat it!"*

I laughed for days. If the only thing standing between me, a marriage license, and a No Vacancy sign on my uterus was a few bites of Caesar salad, why would I not *just eat it?*

I was similarly contrary with the rest of the men I dated during this period, perfectly decent fellows who interested me not at all.

Frequently, out on a date with another guy, I'd notice something and immediately think, "Oh, I can't wait to tell that to Frank." But as Frank continued to enjoy his single life, I started to consider the possibility that I might not marry or have children after all. I started to think it might even be okay. I had discovered work I cared about. I could support myself.

I decided to stop the race to the altar. Stop humiliating myself. Stop going to parties I didn't want to go to, stop trying to enumerate the admirable qualities in men who left me cold. Enough. Included in this resolution was my relationship with Frank. I had let one inappropriate relationship go on too long. I did not want to make that mistake again. Sorry, I told him. I wish you the best. Moving on.

What is it with men? Suddenly, whenever I picked up the phone, it was Frank. A cute postcard in the mail? Frank. Was I free for theater? Movies? Dinner? Eight weeks after I said "See ya," I was spending every night at his apartment.

As the months went by, Mom began to pressure me for a chance to meet him, to check him out for herself. For one thing, she was highly suspicious of his pedigree. "I've never heard of a Jewish man named Frank," she informed me. "And to be named Frank Rich, Jr.? Jews don't have juniors! It's against the religion!"

"His father's side are German Jews, which means they like to pretend they're goyim," I explained. "That's why he's a junior. And it's not Frank like Frank Sinatra. It's Frank like Anne Frank. It's a family name." She wasn't pacified for long. I arranged a dinner for the four of us at Shun Lee West, near Lincoln Center. See? He likes Chinese food. Of course he's Jewish!

And of course she loved him. She loved that we had so much to say to each other, that we enjoyed each other's company, that he was kind to me, and supportive. Unlike my parents and the serial fiancé, Frank wanted us to spend all our time together, whenever we could. I was surprised to find I liked it. We never ran out of conversation. We were married the following year.

After that, Mom would ask me regularly, "How's Frank?" When I told her, she would watch my face more than listen to my answer. Whatever she saw made her nod her head. It was a marriage that looked nothing like hers. She seemed to like the idea of it, at least. Once, I was away with her for the weekend, writing a piece about the Beverly Hills Hotel. I was on the phone with Frank for long stretches. "You just talked to him," she said crankily. "What else is there to say?"

I saw then how much she missed me. I think she was glad I had extricated myself from the penny dreadful that she, my father, and I enacted regularly, and that I'd managed to scrape together enough of myself to forge an actual relationship with someone else. I think she was genuinely happy I found a soul mate. It had never occurred to her to even look for one.

A month after Frank and I married, his mother was severely injured in a car crash. After lingering in a coma for another month, she died on the day we were to move into our new apartment. Frank went to Washington to make funeral arrangements and write a eulogy, and I was left alone to field phone calls from office, family, and friends while also trying to arrange for Nat to be pulled out of sleepaway camp in Maine and flown to D.C. In the midst of all that, I looked at two movers holding a couch that clearly couldn't make it through the doorway and started to shake. I called Phoebe, who was working then as an assistant in a gallery. She listened to me for all of ten seconds before she grabbed her bag and came to help me.

As we'd gotten older, Phoebe and I had become true friends. From time to time, I could be overbearing and she could be ditzy—our childhood roles—but we were loyal to each other, constant and true. I was used to being big sister and substitute Mom, but over time I came to depend on her advice and appreciate her support as much as she appreciated mine. At a certain point, we'd figured out that Mom wasn't always right; we cherry-picked her advice accordingly.

In our aspirations, we remained as different as we'd always been. After finishing college, Phoebe took the post-graduate Sotheby's course in London, but she ultimately lost interest in creating a career in the art world. She held a variety of jobs, but she didn't seem to love any of them. It still wasn't career she cared about; it was children.

I, on the other hand, still felt no rush to procreate, even now that I was in my thirties and married. I was reeling from the good fortune of finding someone to share my life with. When I finished writing a piece at nine o'clock at night, I didn't especially want to settle down next to the baby monitor. I wanted to go out with Frank and maybe some friends, have a drink and some dinner, and yak until I felt like going to bed. Mom was not a fan of this school of thought, but she stopped pushing quite so hard on the children thing. "If you have them and something goes wrong, I don't want you to blame it on me," she concluded.

By coincidence, Phoebe found an apartment around the corner from mine. She stayed only a few years and I didn't fully appreciate the luxury of proximity at the time, but we saw each other often, flopping into bed in one apartment or the other, gabbing, watching TV. She confided in me about her jobs and the guys she was dating, and we spent every Emmy or Grammy or Oscar show on the phone together dishing the clothes.

During this period, she adopted Romeo, a stray kitten who had been abandoned on the West Side Highway, and who spent the first few weeks cowering under her bed. Mom was furious about this; with Phoebe's checkered employment history, Mom felt she hadn't proved responsible enough to take care of herself, let alone a cat. The three of us were at Mom's one night when they had an awful blowout. Phoebe gathered forces and stood her ground. She wanted that cat, she loved that cat. She would not be swayed.

One of the jobs she had during this period was in film production, which is where she met Learan, whom she would eventually marry, though they moved in together without any talk of marriage. Mom went crazy again. Phoebe weathered it. She was tougher than she looked. Like Mom, she didn't express all of her feelings. I expressed every feeling I had at the moment I was having it, and she was remarkably patient about that. She listened. She was resolutely on my side.

Meanwhile, I was getting to know Nat and Simon. They came to our apartment every weekend, though I suggested to Frank that he keep their Wednesday dinners a boys-only tradition. Gradually, Nat and Simon and I formed a relationship all our own. When I was growing up, I'd been desperate to have a third person to turn to when Mom or Dad disappointed me simultaneously. Sometimes that person was Kiki, but often I just felt alone. Now I had a chance to become that person for these boys. It felt right to me. And enough.

When I was single, I almost never cooked for myself. The prospect depressed me. I grew up in a family where food was made in large quantities and leftovers were an integral component of lunches and snacks. The act of buying two lamb chops or using a quarter of a box of pasta was a ringing indictment of my lonely single life: No one would even eat with me!

Once I got married and chose to live in a city apartment rather than a suburban house, I couldn't stockpile food products like Mom, as I didn't have a basement or garage with a full-sized freezer (though there are often spare rolls of paper towels stowed beneath the beds). The freezer way of life never appealed to me, anyway, and mine and Frank's is devoted mostly to vodka, coffee beans, and bagels. There are markets on almost every corner in my neighborhood that sell fresh produce, and I buy as much as we need at a time. I have no doubt that the apocalypse is right around the corner, I just don't feel a need to cater it.

Whereas meals at Mom's were tightly circumscribed by the strictures of keeping kosher, the kitchen I made with Frank is a paean to possibility. We have Indian ingredients, Mexican, Chinese, Japanese, Italian. For the years when Nat and Simon were with us every weekend, Frank and I both cooked. Whenever I made something the kids liked, they wanted it over and over again, and the act of cooking familiar foods became as comforting as eating them. When I made something new and it wasn't very good, Frank didn't mind; it's the thought that counts. It was okay to screw up—to him, if not to me.

I loved sharing my culinary liberation with Mom when she ate with us. Shrimp scampi! Sirloin steak! Followed by a cheese course! For me, "Let's try it" was a happier way to live than "That's not allowed."

But although I cooked differently from the way Mom did, the osmosis she had counted on when I watched her was real. The ballet of bending and stretching for the appropriate pots or platters sets itself in motion, and all you need to do is follow along. Measure a cup of rice, notice how little is left, add it to the shopping list. Sip my drink—Maker's Mark and soda on the rocks, in the same kind of wineglass Mom and Sandy and I used to drink vodka and grapefruit juice from. Talismans of safety.

Peer from the window at the traffic squeezing itself out of the city along the Hudson, and feel flush in knowing I am already home. Stir onions in the pan with a wooden spoon left by a long-vanished roommate. Half watch, half listen to whatever news is on the small TV near the stove, while tapping out my spices in little multicolored heaps. Hear the water boiling for pasta without having to see it, smell when to turn down the heat under the onions. In my kitchen, where every gesture is small and distinct and insignificant to the world beyond my door, I am at peace.

By the spring of 2007, Mom had not improved. The second PET scan Goldstein had suggested to test for Alzheimer's—to show if the damage in her brain was progressive—had come back negative. I was overjoyed. That meant there was still a chance that she could get better.

Around Passover, the family rallied. Mom had taken over making the seder years before, going all out with the china, crystal, and silver. She made a roast turkey and brisket, because two entrées are more festive than one. This year, because she couldn't do the cooking, the kids would do it instead. Greg, Phoebe, and I went up to Scarsdale that afternoon.

When we arrived at one o'clock, Mom had already set the table. It was beautiful, needing only wineglasses and a few things on the seder plate for us to fill in. Learan, Phoebe's husband, is a great cook, as is Greg, and they stormed the kitchen to get the turkey and brisket going. When Mom scurried in anxiously behind them, they told her not to worry, the cooking was in hand. She insisted she could do it herself. Okay then, I said. While they start the other stuff, why don't you make the charoses? Where were the apples, honey, and walnuts? Where were those ingredients? She looked puzzled. Then she opened the refrigerator and started examining the jars in the door.

"Mom, never mind," I said, pulling her into the dining room. "Let's put out the wineglasses. It's the only thing we're missing on the table." But where were they? Only three stood in their usual place. We spent the next hour opening cabinets and drawers all over the apartment, assembling a motley selection. Apparently, whenever one had broken, she had forgotten to replace it. When Learan asked for a carving knife, a similar hunt ensued.

I opened a small chest of drawers near the dining room and was surprised to find all her leather gloves there, instead of in her dresser, second drawer down on the left. With them were a beat-up Kit Kat bar and some small jewelry boxes, most of which were empty. One held a quarter. "What's this about?" I asked Mom.

She looked bewildered. "I don't know."

We went back into the dining room, where she began to reset the table. "Mom, it's perfect, you don't need to do that," I said. Ignoring me, she circled the table for the next hour, studiously moving one place setting to another to another, before sagging into a chair, exhausted. Greg walked her into the den and sat her down with her grandchildren, Phoebe's Ilan and his own son, Dylan, who were both three. Mom looked miserable. She wanted to be in the kitchen. There was company in her house. She was not a guest, she was the host.

When the seder finally started, she and Dad took their seats at either end of the table. A few prayers in, Ilan and Dylan ran into the dining room, yelling, as three-year-olds are wont to do. Mom lost it. "Be quiet!" she shouted.

I thought Phoebe might actually strangle her. "Calm down," I told her. "Mom's upset. She's had a long day." Given Mom's philosophy of child rearing, the shouting itself wasn't a surprise; it was the tenor of the shouting. She'd responded to them not as an adult but as a peer, as if she were frightened that if they didn't quiet down, she might get in trouble, too. She seemed just as small and helpless as they did. She wanted to yell, too.

By that point, we all did. I was finding, eighteen months in, that the day-to-day effort it took to control my temper and my terror in the face of Mom's illness was becoming debilitating. When your beloved parent asks you "What's doing?" the first time, you answer. The third time, you answer. The fifth time you change the subject, the seventh time you go for the booze. My social graces were wearing thin, no matter who asked the questions. Two glasses of wine with dinner became three glasses. Or four. The edge of numbness was a happier alternative to the white-hot center of impotence and rage. Graceless and brusque replaced warm and expansive.

Around that time, Frank and I went out to dinner with a couple we knew and another man. Frank had known the couple long before he and I were married, and together we got on well enough that they'd had us to their summer home and their children's weddings. As these things happen, though, I always preferred the husband to the wife, whom I found silly—selfish and over-indulged. She was the kind of person who never wore a watch, then would turn up late for every engagement, interrupting the conversation to ask, "Am I late?" She did that this very evening. Then she wanted me to go outside and have a cigarette with her. Normally I would have, but not in thirty-degree wind. I said no, a word this woman did not regularly hear. We kept talking, and I could see her misunderstand something I said, taking offense where none was intended. I clarified my point. She willfully ignored me, assuming a wounded air and speaking only in mono-syllables, setting the stage for a Big Scene. I didn't bite.

What I should have done was phone her the next day. Reassure her. Keep track of it. But I was so sick of keeping track, following up, being the grown-up in every single situation, that I dug in and refused to do it. She wanted drama, let her make it. Which she did. We don't speak to this day.

I shouldn't have thought about it for five minutes; this woman was never truly my friend. But as stubborn as I was about not repairing the breach, I still felt as though the failure was mine. The idea that my mother's illness was taking a toll was anathema to me. I could deal with everything just fine. Couldn't I?

Though this was the only "friend" I lost during this awful period, I also lost my memory. Just like that. Frank would tell me about his day and minutes later, I would ask him about it again. I would be sure I sent an e-mail I had written only in my head. I would walk into a room in my apartment, then stop and search for a clue as to why I was there. If Mom wasn't coming back to me, I would go to her, instead. We could still be together—after a fashion.

She and I saw Goldstein in July, after the CT scan from March. His theory was that Mom's depression was exacerbating her problems with concentration and cognition. The strokes had caused "insidious damage to her cognitive and emotional regulation," he said, referring to the fact that Mom was crying—all the time. "Emotional incontinence," he called it. She winced. The very term *incontinence* both frightened and humiliated her, the loss of control the ultimate degradation.

"A lack of enriched structure is making things worse," Goldstein told her. "You need activities to look forward to. Depriving the brain of pleasure affects brain chemistry. I can't fill the tank enough with these pills. Both your mood and memory are not as good now as they were even in March."

That meant back to the drawing board on activities. "Absolutely!" Roberta trumpeted, undaunted, when I called her. She contacted the Botanical Gardens in the Bronx to see if Mom might volunteer there. Mom said no. By that point, I wasn't sure how much of her resistance was anger that she couldn't live the way she had before or simple fear of the unknown. But she remained the obdurate opposite of "positive thinking" or "Do something constructive." She would not try anything new, she would not cooperate. She would hold her breath and still not fall over. And there wasn't a damn thing I could do about it.

Late that June, Phoebe gave birth to her second son, Tal. Mom spent five hours at the hospital, sitting with Phoebe, holding Tal. I joined them and was glad to see Phoebe happy and relaxed.

Like me, Phoebe had gotten married in her early thirties. Unlike me, she tried getting pregnant immediately, and immediately had trouble. She'd given birth to Ilan in 2004 after undergoing eight in vitro fertilizations. For someone who'd intensely wanted children, the repeated failure of the procedure was unnerving. Getting pregnant was such an easy, normal thing—how was it that everyone could do it but her? The stress took a toll on our relationship, which surprised and hurt me. She seemed to withdraw, and when we did speak, the communication was no longer easy and freewheeling. A bout of postpartum depression didn't help. Nor did her attempts at having a second child, which, unfortunately, were just as difficult as the first. It seemed particularly heartbreaking that her hard-won motherhood had collided with the emergence of Mom's dementia. Unfairly and unexpectedly betrayed by her own body, Phoebe had also been unfairly and unexpectedly abandoned by her mother.

The day after Tal's birth, Roberta had an appointment with Mom. They'd continued their sessions, but the through line was dissipating; at each session my mother could no longer remember what they had spoken about during their last. This time Roberta had congratulated her on her new grandson. "She didn't know what I was talking about," Roberta told me.

Phoebe had Tal's bris on July 4. I took the subway to her home near the South Street Seaport. It was very hot and I wore a sleeveless dress and flip-flops. The subway exit I habitually used was closed for the holiday, so I took one unfamiliar to me. Reorienting myself outside, I started toward her apartment building. Walking down the middle of a cobblestone street, I took in the bright sunny day, barely noticing the puddles left by the previous night's rainfall. I looked down, just as I was about to step square on a dead rat, which lay waterlogged in front of me. I froze, my bare toes inches from this bloated rodent, its own hairs standing on end, and felt gripped with horror. It was the worst possible omen: biblical, mafia, and tabloid, all at once. Something was terribly, organically wrong. When I got to Phoebe's house all was well there, but no matter how I tried, I couldn't shake that feeling.

I found myself anticipating disaster at every turn. Not burn-the-house-down disaster, nothing as lofty as that. I worked small. As a counterpoint to my newfound memory loss, I began to lose my clothes. Frank and I had a romantic date night early that summer at the Café Carlyle. I wore a sleeveless black dress and carried a black shawl. Two days later, I panicked. I may have carried it, but now it was gone. I called the Carlyle. It was not in the lost and found. I called the restaurant where we had gone to dinner. Not there, either. I had looked in my closet before, but now I tore through it again, dropping each hanger on the floor, as I went. There was the shawl, neatly folded. It had been there the whole time.

Later that summer, we took a vacation in northern California. One night we met friends for dinner. It was cool in the evenings, so I brought my favorite black sweater to drape around my shoulders as we sat in the restaurant's courtyard. The next day, more panic. Gone. It must have fallen off the back of my chair. I called the restaurant. Nothing. I opened the drawer I had opened three times and looked again. There it was, also neatly folded.

Next came hallucinations. Or, to be specific, one hallucination: Dr. Goldstein. I started seeing him wherever I went. At a friend's memorial service, I spotted him across the room, talking to a woman I knew. As I approached, the woman introduced me. It was not Dr. Goldstein at all. It was someone I had never met before. Then I saw Dr. Goldstein on television. How odd that he would be on the national news, I thought, turning up the volume. Maybe they were doing a story on dementia. No, they were doing a story on the Supreme Court, and John Roberts, Jr., was walking across a stage, shaking someone's hand. Fooled again.

Caroline called. She heard Mom on the phone one day, giving her credit card number to someone. Who was that someone? I never found out because Mom couldn't remember, but we put up big signs near each telephone to remind her not to give out her information. Also around that time, I fired her trainer, a young man she quite liked. He was an enterprising fellow who came to the apartment, spent half an hour doing stretches with her, then billed her for an hour. He also billed her for days he didn't show up. Kiki, who had long balanced Mom's checkbook, had now taken over paying her bills. She was the one who figured out the scam, with help from Caroline, who started keeping records. It wasn't news that some people were glad to take advantage of older people who are easily confused. But it reinforced the feeling that Mom's world was shrinking even more.

Adjustments aside, her medications still weren't right. Dad called to say that when he returned from work one day there was a dinner on the table, another dinner in the oven, and a third dinner on the stovetop. As Mom started preparing one, she seemed to have forgotten it and moved on to the next.

That Thanksgiving, our family planned to hold separate celebrations, which we'd done once before. Even though Nat and Simon were adults, they voluntarily alternated each year between our house and their mom's. When it was our turn two years earlier, they'd wanted to bring additional friends and girlfriends. I couldn't turn up at Phoebe's apartment with seven extra people, so I'd cooked at our place, and planned to do it the same way again.

As Mom always had, I made the recipe for roast turkey given to us by David, our hairdresser of twenty years, who had recently died. David was a Brazilian diva with a dry wit, and I adored him. When he finished my highlights, he'd survey his handiwork, snap off my cape, and say, "Blond again, honey." He loved to cook and we loved his turkey. He would marinate it in red wine, herbs, and spices for twenty-four hours before roasting it. The wine discolors the breast meat, but the bird tastes terrific. David told Mom she could use white wine instead, but once she did something that worked, she never changed it again.

Somehow, the notion of bounty got stuck in my head and short-circuited. Along with the eighteen-pound turkey, I made a Bobby Flay recipe for sweet potatoes mashed with chipotle chilis.

For eight people, I made ten pounds of potatoes. (What I really wanted was the potato kugel that Nana and then Aunt Marcia used to make, but it exerted none of the Proustian pull on Frank and the kids that it did on me—they never loved it.) The stuffing was cornbread, chorizo, and kale—two pans' worth—and my friend Bobby brought Brussels sprouts and dessert. For appetizers, there was smoked salmon on brown bread with dill and, in keeping with the traditions of Mom's house, chopped liver with crackers and chunks of salami with deli mustard for dipping. My apartment smelled delicious, and I was feeding people who all actually liked one another. What could go wrong?

The phone rang on cue.

It was Phoebe. Ilan had been sick the past few days, and she had just come from the doctor. Scarlet fever. She was canceling her dinner. "Do you want Mommy to come to your house?" she asked tersely.

Her question was complicated by the fact that, complaints aside, my father wasn't speaking to me at the time; I think he wasn't speaking to me for two years. When Mom had gotten sick and I mobilized forces, he was appreciative. But when she didn't get better, he was peeved. As far as he could see, this illness amounted to a lot of food being wasted.

I tried focusing on the logistics of the situation rather than the emotional quicksand of it. Obviously, Mom couldn't drive herself to the city. I was pretty sure Dad would drive her if I asked, but I knew he wouldn't come upstairs for dinner; as a child, when he was mad at Nana, he would refuse to eat her food, and he still had that card to play. I knew that his absence would upset Mom and she would spend the whole time worrying about where he was. The entire evening would be hijacked.

"No," I said. I hung up and opened the oven to check the turkey. It was suddenly vital to me that it be perfect. I decided to turn it over to brown it on all sides. One twist, and I succeeded in ripping off half the breast skin, maiming the centerpiece of my holiday meal.

Bobby assured me that all I needed to do was serve it sliced. Who would care? He and his partner, Tom, wrestled it out of the pan, sliced it perfectly, and presented it as if it were going to be photographed. Everything was delicious, and the guests were amused by the sheer volume of food.

But that night I barely slept. Ten pounds of sweet potatoes? I've never even liked sweet potatoes. Only half were eaten. Two pans of stuffing? Only one was eaten. I was cooking for a fantasy family of twenty ravenous phantoms, entwined in both our love for one another and a hatred of leftovers. This notion that food heals, food is magic, food unites, was a fraud. On this holiday, food was a mask, a diversion, one of those fancy football plays people hooted at on television. You got faked out looking at it, cooking it, and thinking about it; all the nasty stuff happened in spite of it. Children got sick, fathers acted out, mothers were left at home without their families. Daughters who liked to think they were organized and powerful enough—and loving enough— to fix their sick mothers channeled their anger and frustration into churning out grub, then couldn't understand that no one else could possibly be as hungry as they were. If I could cook enough magnificent food, it would heal the scar tissue in my mother's brain and cure her depression. It would restore my father's sense of equilibrium and return his wife of fifty-two years to her former glory, and the only thing scrambled in their house would be his eggs, just the way he liked them. It would make my sister have more babies and be my friend again.

That was an awful lot to expect from a sack of sweet potatoes, and even ten pounds of them could not get the job done. Thanksgiving, a holiday I had always loved and looked forward to, ended up being nothing more than a day of majestically bad behavior costumed in the splendor of excess—a mass tantrum cloaked in gravy.

The next morning I got up before seven and headed into the kitchen, still overrun with dirty dishes. I unloaded the dishwasher, reloaded the dishwasher, cleared the sink. I looked out the window at the early morning sunlight and replayed the dinner in my mind. Happy faces, emptied plates, laughter, plenty of thanks. It seemed like a movie that happened to someone else. I moved the roasting pan into the sink, pulling out handfuls of gelatinous onions from the bottom. I felt something else and yanked. There was the missing breast skin, a rectangle of deep golden brown. I held it up to the light and it glinted like stained glass on Sunday. I threw it back in the pan. And crawled back into bed.

David's Roast Turkey

1 (10- to 12-pound) turkey
Garlic powder
Dried oregano
Dried basil
Dried parsley flakes
Salt and pepper
½ bottle red wine
2 medium onions and 1 large onion

One day ahead, rinse and dry the turkey, removing giblets and liver. Generously sprinkle all the seasonings inside and out, rubbing them into the skin. Place the turkey in a double layer of plastic trash bags and add the wine. Close the bags securely with rubber bands and place in the refrigerator. Let marinate for 24 hours, turning periodically.

Preheat oven to 400°F. Slice the 2 medium onions into rings and scatter them in a large roasting pan. Transfer the bird from the double bag to the pan, adding about half the marinade. Cut the large onion in quarters and stuff it into the turkey cavity.

Cover the pan with foil and roast for 30 minutes. Baste, then add one cup of water and cover again. Reduce temperature to 350°F and roast for another 2 hours, basting occasionally.

Remove the foil and roast until done, basting frequently and adding additional water to pan as needed; legs should move easily and skin should be brown, and a thermometer inserted into the deepest part of the thigh should register 175°F. (Depending on your oven and the size of the bird, this might require 30 to 90 minutes additional roasting time.)

Serves 8

Nana's Potato Kugel

....

This recipe comes courtesy of Aunt Marcia.

>   3 pounds all-purpose potatoes, peeled
>   2 medium onions or 1 large onion
>   3 eggs, beaten
>   1 teaspoon baking powder
>   3 ½ teaspoons kosher salt
>   ½ teaspoon black pepper
>   1 cup matzo meal
>   5 tablespoons canola oil

Preheat oven to 400°F. In a food processor, finely grate the potatoes along with the onions in batches.

Transfer mixture to a large bowl and add the eggs, baking powder, salt, and pepper; mix well. Stir in the matzo meal and blend well.

Put 3 tablespoons of canola oil in a 9 by 13-inch glass baking dish and coat the bottom; use a piece of wax paper to spread the oil up the sides. Pour in the batter and smooth the top with a knife. Drizzle the remaining 2 tablespoons of oil on top (you will have excess oil in the corners, but it cooks out).

Bake for 1 hour, until golden brown on top or until a toothpick inserted in the middle comes out clean.

Serves 6

Six

· ● · · · · ·

The holiday season dragged on. When I visited Mom, Caroline handed me a pile of unanswered Christmas cards. Most were from former students; some contained pictures of babies and toddlers. "Look how nice these are," I enthused. "Are you going to answer them?"

"Maybe."

I picked one up. "Do you remember this woman?"

Mom glanced at the picture. "I don't know."

"We can buy some cards, you can dictate, and I can write them for you," I offered.

She peered at the pile. "I don't think so."

"Well," I said. "My mother raised me to answer people when they wrote to me."

She looked me in the eye. "Then I'm glad I wasn't raised by your mother." She put the cards away, and neither of us mentioned them again.

It was definitely time to see Goldstein. We sat in the waiting room opposite a poster titled "Understanding Stroke." "It's enough that I have it—I don't want to understand it," Mom said, turning her back on the other patients, some of whom were in wheelchairs. Her voice escalated. "Do all these people know I've lost half my mind? I don't look like them, do I?"

I grabbed her hand. "They don't know a thing about you, and please don't shout. They've had strokes, but they're not deaf." I pulled a dog-eared issue of *Time* from the table in front of us and put it in her hands. She started reading an article about Hillary Clinton.

"What does it say?" I asked after a few minutes.

"I don't know."

"What do you mean? You've just been reading it."

She put it down. "I start reading something," she said haltingly, "but by the time I get to the end of a paragraph, I can't remember how it started."

By the time we were seated in Goldstein's office, I felt frantic. By tacit agreement during these appointments, I usually remained silent while he and Mom spoke; then he and I e-mailed each other afterward. But this time I repeated what my mother had said in the waiting room. He looked questioningly at her.

She took a deep breath. "It's hard for me to grasp it long enough to be held," she said.

He explained how cerebrovascular disease can splinter thinking and affect language as well. Each of Mom's strokes had left scar tissue in the exact spot in the brain that intensifies depression, which in turn disrupts concentration. The scar tissue, he said, was like a finger pressing on a doorbell—no letup.

That sounded unfixable. He mentioned electric shock treatments, which might help the depression but could scramble her cognition further. Or we could keep trying to find a pharmaceutical balance between stimulating her mind and freaking her out.

"I vote for that," I said. Mom agreed. He switched the medications again.

Two weeks later, I got an early-morning call from Dad to say that Mom had fallen out of bed and hit her head on the night table. Caroline drove her to meet me at Mount Sinai, where Goldstein arranged a CT scan of her brain. More than half her face was already black and blue, even though the point of contact was clearly the red bump above her left eye. The blood thinners she took to prevent more strokes made the bruising swift and dramatic.

The waiting room was large and crowded. CNN droned in a corner. People pulled themselves in tight, flinching when their names were called. Mom was agitated. After five minutes, she wanted to leave. "Why are we here?" she asked fretfully.

"Because you fell out of bed and hit your head."

Maybe ten seconds passed. "Why are we here?"

I remembered the months before Grandma had died, twenty-five years earlier. Sometimes she would call our house every few minutes. "Grandma," I would snap, with the infinite patience of youth and health, "you just called. What is it?" She would cry. "I don't know," she'd say. Then she'd hang up and call back.

"Why are we here?"

An older man sitting next to Mom shifted away, as if whatever she had might be contagious. I pulled a compact from my bag and opened it. "That's why," I said, holding the mirror to her blackened face.

The CT scan was normal. We moved the night table away from her bed in case it happened again. About a week later, the phone rang. It had gotten so my stomach dropped at the sound. "Hello?" I braced for the inevitable blow.

"Hi, Alex. Caroline here."

"Yes?" I started to mentally rejigger the day's schedule.

"Your mom is making her tuna fish," she reported, and laughed.

I was shocked. "She remembers how?"

My mother's tuna fish is her signature dish and my favorite. When I was little, it was tuna with mayonnaise, lemon juice (ReaLemon reconstituted lemon juice, to be exact), and a hard-boiled egg. As I got older, she added canned salmon, celery salt, dill, and salt and pepper—the idea apparently being that two salts are better than one, which, of course, they are. The bread evolved, too, through the years, from Wonder to a brown "health" bread that tasted part whole grain, part pumpernickel. With the pink filling and the green leaf of lettuce, it made a beautiful sandwich.

The last time I'd had it was before she got sick. She'd left one with David at the beauty parlor, knowing I had an appointment with him later in the day. Attached to the brown paper bag was a slip of blue paper that read *Love You Mom*. I still keep both the bag and note in a wire basket in my office so it will retain its shape, as if the sandwich is still inside. I want it to stay the way it was when she left it for me that last time.

When I went to visit the day after Caroline's call, there really was tuna fish again, sheer perfection. I feasted on it, basking in the misplaced faith that it was a sign: Everything would be okay now, the way it was before.

I had brought Mom a copy of my second novel, *The Spare Wife*. Much as I always enjoyed reading fiction, I had never planned on writing it. But I once heard a well-known novelist say that if there's a circus on your front lawn, you have no choice but to write about it. It seemed clear to me that a serial fiancé qualified as a circus, and I used the denouement of that relationship as the basis of my first novel, *Me Times Three*. Writing it had been a cathartic and satisfying experience. So much so that I'd felt emboldened to try fiction again, this time with an omniscient narrator instead of first-person. Learn something new, as Mom always advocated.

The form proved difficult for me—somewhere Stanley Elkin was saying "I told you so"—and between my work at the *Times* and prolonged detours to manage Mom's medical care, I delivered the book two years late. Other writers had warned me that a second novel is always tougher than the first, so I'd taken my setbacks in stride. Or thought I had. But when I read the decidedly mixed review in *The New York Times Book Review*, I felt slammed. A few nights later, Frank and I went to see a Broadway revival of one of my favorite musicals, Stephen Sondheim's *Sunday in the Park with George*, about the artist Georges Seurat. I started to cry in the first act and didn't stop even when the show had ended.

We went out for a bite and I kept crying. Frank was alarmed. Trying to answer his questions, I barely managed to sob out a line from the play. It was from the scene when Seurat and his mother sit on the island of La Grande Jatte, where he made his landmark painting. She sings about how much the things around them have changed. "Oh, Georgie," she finally exclaims with great sadness, "how I long for the old view."

Well, that made two of us.

My mother took the book from me and oohed and aahed. She told me how proud she was. She would read it immediately, she promised.

"Really?" I asked. "Can you do that?"

"Why not?" she answered, looking offended.

Of course Mom couldn't read my book. I knew she couldn't. What took me longer to realize, as other reviews appeared, both good and bad, was that somehow I had set up this book as a test. Finishing it had run parallel to seeking a cure for my mother. By the time it was done, she would be cured, I thought. If I got an A on the book it would mean I had fixed her; I would be perfect, and so would she. But I had finished the book, it was not perfect, and she was not cured. I had done my best—that slick old excuse—and it hadn't worked. The one person I wanted most to read my book could not. She couldn't read at all. I had failed on every count. Never before had I experienced a failure that Mom couldn't mitigate, or a victory that Mom couldn't celebrate.

The desolation of it overwhelmed me. I stopped sleeping, listening hour after hour to the sounds of the highway outside my window, the intermittent screech of brakes, then counting—one second, two, three—until the crash. Or sometimes worse, the silence. What happened? Finally, at five-fifteen a.m., came the rumble of the first bus up Riverside Drive. It was the one thing that put me to sleep. Maybe because it was so reliable. I imagined the people getting on, going to work, beginning their day. I shrank from mine. It didn't feel as if it mattered that much.

A few weeks later, a good friend threw me a dinner party to celebrate the book's publication. The food was delicious and the guest list was mine. I was surprised to find that I thoroughly enjoyed myself and felt better than I had in months.

Early the next morning, the phone rang. "I have breast cancer," Phoebe said without preamble. "I need a doctor." It was three days before she would turn forty-one. Ilan was four, Tal eight months old.

"Wait," I said. "What happened?" She told me the story of getting a mammogram, of the technician looking at the films and Phoebe seeing on her face that it was bad. She had known something was wrong, she said. She'd felt a lump under her arm.

I started working the phones. Whatever the tensions between us, there was no question of my rallying to help her. That evening, she and I drove to Scarsdale so she could tell our parents. We walked in on them having dinner. Mom sobbed. Dad asked questions. I drank Maker's Mark. Phoebe held herself together like a champ, in ironclad emergency mode.

The next day, I called Mom to see how she was taking it.

"It was so nice to see you last night," she said.

"What do you mean?"

"You came up here last night."

"Yes, to tell you that Phoebe has breast cancer."

She screamed. "She does?"

Later that day I went to Brooklyn to meet with the food writer Arthur Schwartz. He was about to publish a book on Jewish home cooking, and he was going to teach me how to make kreplach so I could write about it for my *Times* column.

I'd come to food writing relatively late, partly because I'd been under the mistaken impression that to write about food professionally, you needed to have cooked professionally. Though many food writers have done that, it turned out not to be required. At the *Times*, I often wrote a feature called "At Lunch With," a snapshot of a celebrity during the span of a meal we'd had together. Over time, there was a wide-ranging cast of characters, everyone from Alec Baldwin to Ed Koch to Omar Sharif. Eventually, the Dining section wanted more food-related stories, which had taken me deeper into the world of cooking.

Chefs and restaurant owners were welcome additions to the entertainment and media figures I generally wrote about. People who feed people are some of the nicest people in the world—their livelihoods depend on it. To sit in the kitchen with them and watch them cook, the same way I used to watch Mom and Nana, felt familiar and safe. Anne Byrn, who writes the wildly successful series of Cake Mix Doctor books, came to my apartment to bake some cakes with me. An hour later, when the cakes were in the oven and we were eating lunch, our conversation had moved seamlessly past hand mixers versus standing mixers to caring for elderly relatives. It felt of a piece, somehow, to share a few confidences along with baking tips. It's what women have done for centuries.

For a profile of the great chef Edna Lewis, who in her later years suffered from Alzheimer's disease, I spent a remarkable afternoon at the home she shared with her protégé, the chef Scott Peacock, outside Atlanta. Miss Lewis, as Scott called her, was wary of me, a stranger she did not recognize. To see Scott draw her out and fuss over her, amid the sights and sounds and smells of their kitchen, until finally she smiled broadly, enjoying her lunch and the company, transcended my job and opened a window onto a familial relationship I had no idea would one day resonate with my own. Kitchens and dining rooms, in homes and in restaurants, are dynamic settings for intricate, dramatic characters, just as the theater is. And you get to eat, too.

As the push for more personal writing grew at the *Times,* in pace with the rest of the world, it felt natural, eventually, to enter the fray. I'm barely brushing my teeth in the morning when I start to think about what's for dinner that night. Although this is surely the sign of a deeply rooted psychological problem, the socially acceptable term for it is "passion." So it was a passion for eating that led to my "Feed Me" column. Unlike profile writing, which is all about seeing someone else, these essays on eating were often idiosyncratic, personal. A piece on making borscht in the summertime resonated with readers, just as the piece on Arthur Gelb and the latkes had. In the midst of a column about a couple who make an annual dairy seder, I included a brief description of Mom at our seder, reaching for the Maalox as she watched someone drop red horseradish on the white tablecloth. That brought its own avalanche of e-mail. The smaller and more specific the subject, I discovered, the more amplified the echo. That engaged me almost as much as the eating.

Aside from a challah-making jag in college, I have never been much of a baker, partly because I've never had much of a sweet tooth, but mostly because I can't stand the pressure. I've always driven myself so hard outside the kitchen that the threat of producing a fallen cake or a leaden loaf discourages me before I begin. But partly because of "Feed Me," I found myself backtracking on my baking stance; there is something inherently generous and healing about making a cake or a loaf of bread, foods made to feed more than one. I baked brownies for the first time in decades, from a superb and simple recipe published by Kate Moses in her memoir, *Cakewalk*. It wasn't stressful at all; the hardest part was waiting for them to cool so I could eat them.

I know I absorbed by osmosis Mom's fear of baking. She so doubted her abilities that she relied almost exclusively on mixes— or the Scarsdale Pastry Center. After a stab at apple pies at Terhune Avenue—overstuffed, unevenly browned, and wildly misshapen—she wised up in later years, filling frozen pie shells with cans of Libby's pumpkin pie mix. They were delicious, actually, and with a dollop of Cool Whip they remain Phoebe's and my favorite Mom dessert of all time.

Some people will sneer at pumpkin pie from a can. I celebrate it. Cooking for people you love is a personal, idiosyncratic undertaking and there is no right or wrong. I keep this in mind when interviewing professional chefs. I never feel ashamed of what I can or cannot make. I am not in competition with them, nor do many of their procedures interest me, except as a spectator sport. My editors and recipe tester at the *Times* collectively cringe when I come up with a column that relies on a professional chef's recipe, and I learned early to cringe along with them. Professional chefs have no real interest in home cooking, and having to translate their measurements to feed four or six is like an extra-credit math question they would rather skip.

The key to home cooking is knowing a good thing when you see it and having the sense to stick to it. If you want to express yourself, buy a pair of chartreuse socks. Don't change the family dinner! There was a time when Mom got the notion of burying hard-boiled eggs inside her meat loaf, so there was egg in every slice. I liked it well enough, but the rest of the family went on strike; they loathed it. I read an article by a food writer recently in which she said she was such a tinkerer by nature that she never made a dish the same way twice. The notion both depressed and unnerved me. I'm all for adventure, but home is about continuity. Some things should never change.

All these years later, Nana's kreplach still possessed me, crisp triangles of fried dough filled with seasoned chopped meat. Mom had never tried to duplicate them, buying them frozen instead. That was better than no kreplach, but hardly the same.

"Lazy," Arthur Schwartz had sniffed when I'd described Nana's kreplach to him. His kreplach were filled with shredded pot roast and crimped together at their ends to make what he called Jewish tortelloni, then boiled and floated in chicken soup. We agreed to have a kreplach throwdown. I cared less about winning than I did about trying to somehow conjure Nana. If I kneaded that dough hard enough, maybe she would appear before me, like a genie with three wishes. One: Cure Mom. Two: Cure Phoebe. Three: Disconnect my phone.

Before our visit, I had read Arthur's *Jewish Home Cooking: Yiddish Recipes Revisited*, which was a direct hit on my childhood memories. When I'd called him initially, I told him Aunt Marcia still kept Nana's kreplach in her freezer. This was in 2008. Nana died in 1968.

"Oh, my refrigerator is filled with dead people's food," Arthur replied casually.

And why shouldn't it be? My brain is filled with dead people's food. Anyone who ever stood in line at Ratner's, the kosher dairy restaurant on the Lower East Side, remembers the onion rolls. A man walked up and down the line handing them out, to stave off hunger and keep you there, waiting for a table. Warm from the oven, they were chewy pillows topped with frizzled onions and poppy seeds, fragrant with the promise of even better things to come. Once seated, I would order my usual—a plateful of mashed potatoes, peas, and mushrooms—which I mixed together into a heap of delectable mush.

That mush technique was also handy for Nana's meatballs. She made wonderful potted meatballs in sweet-and-sour sauce, another recipe Arthur had in his book, and I just loved them. She served them with rice on the side, never spaghetti, and you could break up the very large meatballs and mix them into the rice with the sauce.

Nana's brother, Coduk, also loved those meatballs. Coduk (pronounced SUD-duk) was actually famous in family lore for an inauspicious reason: He wasn't smart. In a Jewish family besotted with education, being a dummkopf was a *shanda,* which in Yiddish means "shame." Coduk was, however, a gifted tailor, and worked at Chipps, a men's clothing store, where he was known as the trouser man. He was also something of a ladies' man—he had quite a beautiful wife—and a legendary dancer. "In his hands and his feet, he's a genius," Dad and Nana would say. I never had a conversation with him—he spoke only Yiddish—but I do remember engaging him in some competitive meatball eating when I was seven or eight. He was matching and raising me until Nana cut me off with "Your eyes are bigger than your stomach," which carried the inglorious sting of truth.

I watched as Coduk continued to eat. In contrast to my penchant for turning all food into baby food, breaking it down and mixing it together, he was an isolationist. He kept his meatballs separated from his rice, which in turn was separated from his spinach. He ate each item sequentially, starting with the meatballs. I couldn't understand the point of eating rice plain when there was sauce to be had. Maybe what they said about him was true.

Included in Arthur's book on Jewish home cooking was a reproduction of a seder menu from the Concord Hotel in 1967. One of our old haunts from the Jewish War Veterans conventions! Seeing that menu was such a time warp. It felt ancient. I felt ancient. But once I was in Arthur's apartment, I knew I'd found a kindred spirit. His kitchen was small and comfortably cluttered, the table jammed near the window. Before attempting the kreplach, we sat and chatted, had some tea. My shoulders moved a full inch down from my ears. When he opened his packed refrigerator, I didn't ask him to show me the dead people's food. I felt like being alive for a while.

Soon enough, we began to cook, rolling out the dough. Or at least he did. It was hard for me to get it thin enough. I could hear Mom's "No manual dexterity!" ringing in my ears. So true— certainly no one would say I had genius in *my* hands. Arthur offered a pasta roller, but I refused. I would do it Nana's way. He browned an onion and some garlic and added the meat to the pan. The aroma was pure childhood. I spooned some of it onto my squares of dough and folded them over. The points of the triangles were too thick, but we fried them anyway. They were good! Too doughy, but for a first try not bad. He hadn't made any soup, so we tried his kreplach fried. Not as good. We tried a version using wonton wrappers. Terrible.

Arthur ceded victory graciously and, for the road, gave me a Tupperware filled with a delicious mock chopped liver from his cookbook, made with green beans, onions, and walnuts. I sat in the subway, the container on my lap, feeling suddenly spent. There had been no visions of Nana, but I had been grateful to sit in a cheerful kitchen with a kindhearted person. It is an intimacy to cook with someone else, inhabit his space. I was moved by it. We had kept company that afternoon.

I needed it.

In the days and weeks that followed Phoebe's diagnosis, I found it hard to keep my head up. Literally. My hands, folded in my lap, were about as much as I could take in. I had difficulty concentrating. I came out of the shower one evening and walked into my bedroom, where the TV was on. It was one of those entertainment programs in which the hosts ask questions about celebrity rumors. "We've got cancer!" one of them announced as I sank onto the bed. *What?* I stared at the set before realizing he had said, "We've got the answer!"

I wished I could say the same. I kept working. I promoted the book. I got back into the habit of speaking regularly to Phoebe—and to her doctors. She and I had been distant for so many of her in vitro years, it was hard to just leap back into a relationship. We crawled.

Later that spring, Dad phoned. "Your mother isn't getting any better," he informed me. "We need a second opinion." Given everything I knew about her condition from Goldstein, I wasn't sure what the point would be. So much damage had been done before we'd even arrived at the scene. Still, what was there to lose? I asked around and got a referral to a neurologist in private practice—an unequivocal "If it were my mother, this is who I would want her to see." When I told Goldstein about the second opinion, he seemed somewhat dismayed, but scrupulously compiled a medical file for us.

In contrast to Goldstein—rumpled and running, whether to patients or students—this older man was polished, reserved. Where Goldstein's office was a spill of thank-you cards and gifts stashed in every corner, this doctor's office was spare, decorated only with pictures of his children, expensively framed. He had a mane of silver hair and wore a blue shirt with a white collar and a yellow tie—a refugee from Wall Street, or a Greenwich country club.

"How do I know you again?" he asked absently as we entered his office. "Who sent you?" As we sat down, he opened the mammoth file Goldstein had assembled and started to read.

The door to the fancy doctor's office stayed open. Privacy didn't seem to concern him. The nurse called in for him to pick up the phone. For a full five minutes, as we sat in front of him, he small-talked, turning the pages of Goldstein's report casually, as if reading a magazine. "Sorry," he said, when he hung up.

"Really," I snorted.

"I had to take that call," he snapped, instantly furious.

He glanced at another page or two of documentation, then at Mom. "Name ten vegetables for me." I gripped the arms of my chair. Was this a joke?

"Potatoes," she started gamely. "Carrots. Peas. Rhubarb. Tomatoes." She faltered. "I think those are fruit, actually."

"Keep going," he droned, eyes down, turning pages. But she'd lost her train of thought.

He suggested we repeat the PET scan. "It's also possible she's had more strokes," he said. "You could do another CT scan." And that, in sum, was the extent of his advice.

As we walked down the block to Caroline's car in a drenching rain, Mom started to cry. I felt like joining her. Once inside, the three of us talked for a while.

"How is Phoebe doing?" Caroline asked. I started to tell her about the treatment.

"What?" Mom howled. "Why didn't I know about this?"

I explained, as gently as I could, that she did know, that Phoebe and I had come up to tell her, that she and I had talked about it since. She wept, heartbroken. "I should never forget something like that," she said. Her voice was filled with sorrow, but her face was filled with dread.

That was the last time any of us mentioned Phoebe's illness in front of her.

The following week, Mom and I went back to Mount Sinai, where Goldstein repeated the PET scan. It was normal again. As was the CT scan. She hadn't had any more strokes. Who was the vegetable now?

As low as I felt during this period, I still wanted to cook. But even though I was fixated on memory, yearning for Nana or Grandma or, most of all, Mom to appear in my kitchen and take me by my child's hand, backward into the glory of the lobby of Grossinger's, I was no longer cooking for connection. I was cooking for distance. I stayed away from Mom's recipes. If I made one, I felt I'd choke on it.

When I was first learning to shop for clothes, Mom told me the idea was never to spend a lot of money but to look as if I had. My approach to cooking is similar: Choose an uncomplicated recipe that is more than the sum of its parts. The people eating it are just as happy as if I'd worked twice as hard. I recently read a recipe, I can't remember for what, because the minute I saw "24 cups of ice" on the ingredient list, I turned the page. Think about that: The act of measuring out those cubes. Then think about an apartment freezer. Then think about opening a jar of peanut butter.

But if I am less than swashbuckling in the kitchen, I have learned through the years to play to my audience. Frank, Nat, and Simon love boldly spiced food, so if a recipe calls for two cloves of garlic, I use six. Though I often make spaghetti carbonara from a Marcella Hazan cookbook, I can assure you she would never recognize the finished product. It is Nat's favorite dish; the way I've adapted it through the years suits our taste. For a pound and a quarter of pasta, she calls for half a pound of pancetta; for two pounds of pasta, I use a pound and a half of bacon. (Howl all you want, I can't hear you.) I use her Italy as my inspiration, and my family loves it.

That's what home cooking is about—shared tastes, mutual passions. Part of the appeal of cooking for family and friends is the absence of being judged. It's private. That's why I'm not an easy entertainer; when I have to cook for people I don't really know or don't really like, I'm miserable. As a writer, my work is out in the world for criticism or praise. I don't want my dinner out there, too. It's mine, and the opinion that counts most about it is mine. The thing that home cooks need to learn is the same thing writers need to learn: You can eat at the best restaurants in the world, just as you can read the great books of the world, but just as you have to write like yourself, when it comes to cooking, you have to cook like yourself.

Simon was coming to dinner one Sunday night, and I wanted to make something he'd love. I sat down with my bulging recipe binder. So many recipes for filet mignon, Mom's favorite. Then there was that two-day lasagna—I was still waiting for an appropriate snowstorm to attempt that one.

Finally, since we all like Indian food, I chose a roasted Indian-spiced leg of lamb, coriander potatoes with spinach, and raita. It was a time-consuming meal to prepare in the way all Indian meals are, not because they're difficult, but because they have so many ingredients. I worked slowly and methodically, using recipes from *Food & Wine*. Leg of lamb is not a kosher cut, so I didn't grow up eating it, but I love how well it plays with others. Just name the herb or spice and it's happy to engage. You want to dress up Indian today? French? Greek? Sure.

I couldn't remember if Mom even liked Indian food. I don't remember her ever eating it. But I knew, as I washed the fresh spinach, that this was a move Mom would disdain. Too much time. She used frozen in her spinach kugel, a noodle pudding that included a trifecta of nightmare ingredients: stick margarine, non-dairy creamer, and Lipton's onion soup mix. In the old days, I could eat a pan of it. For this dish, however, frozen spinach was too watery, and fresh gave it a better color.

The dinner was a resounding success. Bravo for *Food & Wine*. Bravo for me. Yet as I washed the mountains of dishes afterward, I tried to pinpoint what exactly I had accomplished. Dinner. That's it. The transcendent comforts of cooking had completely escaped me. I followed some recipes and the result was that some very tasty food was cooked and consumed. There was no healing, no salvation. My sister still had cancer and my mother still had dementia.

And I still couldn't accept either of those facts. All I wanted to do was go back.

In July, I took Mom to Lord & Taylor in Eastchester, near Scarsdale, for shopping and lunch, a throwback to our old life together. Bonwit Teller had been in that shopping center. I. Miller Shoes. A bookstore, I think Brentano's. Now there was Nike.

I had gotten Mom to agree to the outing with the promise of a Clinique gift bag, another remnant of the old days, and one she seemed to remember. We headed inside and made a beeline to the Clinique counter. Samples? There were none that day. Slightly dispirited, we wandered toward pocketbooks. I'd had the same one for at least a dozen years, I told Mom. Disgraceful, really.

"You always have trouble buying bags," Mom said offhandedly, as if we'd talked about this yesterday. I looked at her. Same clouded expression, same uncertain gait. But that comment came from some part of her brain that was still alive. She was right. I've had trouble buying bags ever since college, when I read in some magazine that small women carrying bags too large for them look like children carrying their mothers' bags. "That look is much too young for her" from our Grossinger's days translated into "That look is much too old for her" when applied to a pocketbook.

We walked toward the elevators, stopping to look at jewelry. I was desperately scanning the cases for a gold circle pin. Mom had given me a beautiful one ages ago, two strands forming the circle, and a year before, I had worn it out to dinner. By the time I got home, it was gone. I hadn't had the heart to tell her.

"Anything here look good to you?" I asked brightly.

She shrugged and turned away. "I don't need anything anymore," she said.

"That's not true," I countered. "Everyone needs something."

She shook her head. "When I shopped, I bought what I liked and what I wanted. I didn't like much and I didn't want much."

I laughed. I was the same.

The one thing we both wanted, always, was to eat. For years, the restaurant at Lord & Taylor was the Bird Cage. I can still taste the "society sandwiches"—shrimp salad, cucumber, chicken, and my favorite, date nut bread with cream cheese. (I can still remember the calorie count, too, for those date nut and cream cheese sandwiches, the highest in the paperback guide I carried around with me in my thigh-obsessed teenage years.)

The store had expanded since then, and the restaurant was now upstairs. It was empty, except for two other tables. It wasn't called the Bird Cage anymore. It was Larry Forgione's Signature Café—and not for long, according to our waitress. All the restaurants in Lord & Taylor stores would soon be Sarabeth's Kitchens. This one was about to close so they could redesign the space, the menu. She didn't know if she would keep her job, she said. On the sunny summer day, the unadorned room felt forlorn.

A flyer listed specials, including a double cheeseburger. For heaven's sakes, who here would order that? We asked for a menu. There they were still, society sandwiches. "Does that sound good?" I asked, and Mom nodded. She knew enough to know that familiar references escaped her, so instead of drawing attention to that fact, she would just acquiesce, hoping to catch up later.

I gave the waitress our order. When she left, Mom leaned across the table. "Give her a good tip, she's old," she said.

The sandwiches came on a naked white plate, ice cold. I hadn't laid eyes on date nut bread since high school and didn't expect to now, so I wasn't disappointed by its absence. We sipped our Diet Cokes and picked up one tasteless triangle at a time. Suddenly, I glimpsed Mom across the table. I saw her come back, inhabit her face. She remembered this was something we had done together before. She had loved it, too. "This is good," she said, and I knew she was not talking about the food.

I fished in my bag for a pen. It occurred to me that I should take notes, and stupidly, I had come unprepared. No pen, no paper. As a reporter, a complete disgrace.

I grabbed the flyer with the daily specials. "You don't have a pen, do you?" I asked, looking to flag the waitress, already knowing the answer. Mom opened her bag and put two pens on the table. Also a pack of tissues and a lipstick.

"Incredible! You are always prepared!"

She blushed, pleased. "I'm a teacher," she said by way of explanation.

I nodded. "My favorite teacher."

We wished the waitress luck on the transition and I left her a generous tip, pointing it out to Mom. She looked blank. "Okay," she said tentatively.

Once home, we made some tea and sat at the dining room table. I lit a cigarette. Mom had stopped smoking once she got sick, but she always asked me to blow some smoke in her direction. My own smoking had dwindled through the years to an average of one cigarette a day. Being my mother's daughter, I could not quit just because I was supposed to.

As I smoked, Mom and I talked some more, until she blurted out, "Don't finish your cigarette."

"Why?" I asked.

She looked like a child. "Because when you finish it, you'll leave."

I promised her I wouldn't, and for another half an hour we sat and talked. I got up to go to the bathroom. When I returned a few minutes later, she was fast asleep at the table. I touched her hand. "Hi there," I said. "Do you want to sit some more or would you like to rest?"

"Maybe rest," she said.

I walked her into the den, where she napped in the afternoon.

She lay down on the couch and I covered her with a blanket. I noticed, on the coffee table, a small transistor radio. The kind that Selig had given her as a child.

"Here you go," I said, handing it to her. I sat next to her while she turned it on and fiddled with the dial. "I can stay here until you fall asleep," I offered, but she shook her head no.

"I'm fine," she said. "Thank you for a wonderful day."

I kissed her. "Thank *you*," I said. "I loved being with you, my sweet Mommy."

"And I loved being with you . . ." She searched for the word "daughter" and couldn't find it. "My big girl," she said. I tucked her in. She put the radio near her ear, her link to the outside world.

My big girl. How I wished those words were true. I had never felt smaller.

The following week, Phoebe had her surgery. The day after, I went to see her at home, bringing lunch. Her mother-in-law, Yael, had taken the kids out and the apartment was quiet. Phoebe looked great. She had that luminous energy that can come after a horror—whether it's adrenaline or relief—though the surgery had gone well.

She lay in her bed and I sat in it beside her. We talked, about the doctor and the hospital, about the kids and Learan, about her boss and her friends. We talked the way we used to, the way sisters talk, some half-private language of coos and cues, comforting noises of possibly no substance or possibly the most important thing you'd ever heard, like an electric current, up and down. I said something, I cannot remember what, and she threw her head back and laughed. It took my breath away to watch her—my little sister who became the smart and funny woman who was also my friend, then somehow slipped away. Here she was again. We were still connected.

I hadn't seen Phoebe laugh in years. I hadn't heard her voice without anger in it for years. She threw her head back and there was a picture, vivid and familiar; the graceful length of her throat, the finely tipped point of her nose, the wide smile of joy.

Finally. The old view.

Arthur Schwartz's Fried Meat Kreplach

FOR THE FILLING:

> 2 tablespoons vegetable oil
> ½ cup minced onion
> 1 small garlic clove, minced
> ½ pound ground chuck
> Salt and freshly ground pepper

FOR THE DOUGH:

> 1 ¾ cups all-purpose flour
> 2 extra-large eggs
> 2 tablespoons water, plus more as needed
> Salt
> Canola oil, for frying
> Applesauce, for serving (optional)

PREPARE THE FILLING:

In a small skillet, heat oil over medium heat. Add onion, and sauté until well browned, 6 to 8 minutes. Toward end of cooking, add garlic and stir well.

Add beef, breaking it up well with the side of a wooden spoon. Sauté until it has lost its raw color. Season with salt and pepper, and sauté another 2 minutes. Remove from heat and let cool.

MAKE THE DOUGH:

Mound flour on a wooden board or in a large mixing bowl. Make a well in the center. Break eggs into well, then add 2 tablespoons lukewarm water. With a fork, beat eggs and water together, incorporating a bit of the flour. As liquids blend, continue to push flour into well until it is all mixed in, drizzling in up to 2 more tablespoons water as needed to make a cohesive dough.

When dough is well blended, mix it by hand, then begin to knead it on a flat surface. With a bench scraper, turn dough and press it with your fingertips, then knead a few strokes again. The dough should become smooth and elastic, remaining only slightly sticky; if it is too sticky, lightly sprinkle work surface with flour and continue to knead. Form dough into a ball and let rest on the board, covered with a bowl or a piece of plastic wrap, for 30 minutes.

MAKE THE KREPLACH:

Divide dough in two and work with one half, keeping the other half covered so that it stays moist. Roll the dough out on a floured board, stretching and turning it, until it is very thin. (Alternately, use a crank-handled pasta machine on thinnest or next-to-thinnest setting.)

Cut dough into 3-inch squares. Put 1 rounded teaspoon of filling in the center of each square. With a brush or a finger, moisten edges of squares with water. Fold dough from corner to corner, forming triangles, and seal carefully.

Bring a large pot of well-salted water to a boil over high heat. Working in batches if necessary, add kreplach—do not crowd pot—and boil until dough is tender and filling is cooked, 6 to 8 minutes. Drain and cool.

Kreplach can be frozen at this point. To use, thaw in refrigerator or at room temperature.

Place a large skillet over medium-high heat and add about
$1/8$ inch canola oil. When oil is simmering, add boiled kreplach.
Fry until well browned and crispy on both sides. Serve hot,
accompanied by applesauce, if desired.

Makes about 2 dozen

Sweet and Sour Potted Meatballs

· ·

Adapted from Arthur Schwartz's Jewish Home Cooking: Yiddish Recipes
Revisited *(Ten Speed Press).*

*If you can get your hands on the sour salt called for in this recipe, use it. It is also
sold as citric acid and is available online from Amazon and King Arthur Flour,
among other suppliers. You can substitute lemon juice, but the meatballs won't have
the same Old World flavor.*

FOR THE SWEET-AND-SOUR SAUCE:

2 tablespoons canola oil
1 medium onion, finely minced
1 (15-ounce) can tomato sauce
$1/2$ cup water
$1/2$ teaspoon sour salt, or the juice of 1 lemon
    (about 2 tablespoons)
$1/4$ cup firmly packed dark brown sugar
Salt and freshly ground black pepper

FOR THE MEATBALLS:

2 pounds ground chuck
2 eggs, beaten
$1/3$ cup long-grain rice, parboiled for 3 minutes
1 cup fresh bread crumbs from challah
1 medium onion, grated on the coarse side of a box
    grater
2 $1/4$ teaspoons salt
$1/2$ teaspoon freshly ground black pepper

PREPARE THE SAUCE:

In a large Dutch oven, heat the oil, then sauté the minced onion over medium heat until tender and golden, 8 to 10 minutes. Add the tomato sauce, and rinse out the can with ½ cup water to loosen any sauce that remains, adding that liquid to the pan. Stir in the sour salt or lemon juice and brown sugar. Bring to a simmer, uncovered, over medium heat. Remove from the heat and set aside.

MAKE THE MEATBALLS:

Put the ground meat in a large bowl and push it to one side. Add the eggs, rice, bread crumbs, onion, salt, and pepper to the other side of the bowl and combine with a large fork. Work in the meat, handful by handful, until everything is thoroughly blended.

Return the sauce to a gentle simmer over medium heat. Using a ½-cup measure to shape them, make meatballs measuring about 2½ inches and drop them gently into the sauce. You should have 10 to 12.

Cover and simmer slowly for 30 minutes, gently rotating and pushing the meatballs around halfway through the cooking so that they are thoroughly coated in sauce after about 15 minutes. Correct seasoning with salt and pepper if necessary.

Serve very hot.

The meatballs not only are fine to reheat, but actually benefit from being left several hours or even overnight in the refrigerator. Store in the covered pot, unless it's not aluminum, and reheat over low heat.

Makes 10—12 meatballs, to serve 4

Spinach Kugel

· ·

> ½ pound medium egg noodles
> 1 package (9 ounces) frozen spinach, thawed and drained
> 3 eggs, beaten
> ½ stick (4 tablespoons) margarine, melted
> 1 cup liquid nondairy creamer (available in frozen food
>   section)
> Vegetable oil spray, such as Pam
> Sweet paprika

Preheat the oven to 350°F.

Bring a large pot of water to a boil and salt liberally. Add the
noodles and cook until tender; drain.

In a large bowl, combine the spinach, eggs, margarine, and
creamer. Add the noodles and mix thoroughly.

Spray an 8-inch-square baking dish with vegetable oil. Add the
noodle mixture and level the top. Sprinkle with paprika. Cover
the dish with aluminum foil and bake on the center rack of the
oven for 40 minutes. Remove the foil and bake, uncovered, for
an additional 10 minutes.

Remove from oven and let stand for 15 to 30 minutes. Cut into
squares and serve.

Serves 4

Seven

· ● · · · · ·

The optimism of September, rich with the anticipation of back-to-school, new clothes, weekend outings, and dress-up parties, was now lost on Mom. Everyone was back to school except her. The Jewish high holidays were no longer a celebration but an obstacle course of rituals she could neither remember nor execute properly. Once again, it seemed her pill regimen had fallen out of sync. When Kiki visited one weekend and went out to dinner with my parents, Mom asked if she and my father were moving.

Still trying to focus her, Goldstein supplemented her antidepressant with a second one. A few weeks passed. On a Thursday afternoon, the day before Halloween, I took the train to Scarsdale to see my friend Philip, who was visiting from Los Angeles. My plan was to check on Mom first.

I hadn't told her I was coming, since her temporal sense was no longer functioning. I realized this over the summer when I'd gone to help her with her garden. She and Dad had downsized to an apartment in the mid-1990s, but she'd carried on with her passion, staking out a slab of rock on a hill behind the building to cultivate a rock garden—because planting a regular garden would have been too easy. I had gone up to work with her two days in a row. On the second day, when I mentioned something we'd planted "yesterday," she had no memory of my being there. On other occasions, when I tried making plans with her in advance (Goldstein's admonition of "Look forward to something" ringing in my ears), she would ask me the time and date repeatedly, becoming more and more anxious about remembering it.

I had been especially worried about her over the past few days since one of the doormen told Caroline that Mom had come to the lobby one morning in her nightgown. "Is someone here for me?" she'd asked him.

I called her from the train around five o'clock. Her voice was muted, tremulous. "What's wrong?" I asked. "You don't sound good."

"I'm not," she said.

When I rang her bell, there was no answer. I called her on my cell phone. "Mom, I'm out front," I said. "Please open the door."

She did, wearing her heavy winter coat, which was buttoned up to her jaw. Her face was red and her hands felt on fire. She was dazed, scared, crying. I helped her remove the coat—she didn't know why she was wearing it—and we walked into the kitchen. A package of frozen chicken sat on the counter, and next to it lay a note: *Can't make dinner,* she had written in a shaky hand. Then the words sloped down the page. *Please help me.*

I hugged her and tried to calm her while calling Goldstein on his cell. He agreed to meet us at Mount Sinai in the morning. I got Mom settled on the couch in the den and stayed there, holding her tight. I called Clark Wolf, whom I was scheduled to see the next day. Clark is a food and restaurant consultant I met in 1988 when I was an editor at *Mirabella.* Part of my job was having monthly lunches with him to get story ideas. He used to tease me for always ordering chopped meat—meat loaf, meat sauce, hamburger, shepherd's pie—and would scan the menu for my "chopped-meat variations."

For years, Clark had been working on a comprehensive book about American cheeses, and I wanted to write about it for my *Times* column. He'd arranged for two chefs to prepare different versions of macaroni and cheese from recipes included in the book. I'd never liked mac and cheese growing up, and still didn't, but he swore these would change my mind. He'd also planned a separate cheese tasting.

I called Clark and told him where I was and what was going on. Clearly, I would have to reschedule. He understood my dilemma completely, but he couldn't reschedule. He was leaving first thing Saturday morning for California, where he was registered to vote, and wouldn't return to New York for weeks. The chefs were lined up to cook the next morning, and the cheeses for our tasting were already purchased.

I channeled the spirit of Roberta Epstein and called Greg to explain the jam I was in. If he could meet me at Sinai the next morning at ten, I could stay there with him and Mom until eleven-thirty, head downtown, eat two kinds of macaroni and cheese in the West Village, run to SoHo for the cheese tasting, and be back uptown by three-thirty. He agreed, while trying not to laugh: "This is your *job*?"

The plan worked. I met Clark on time and was back at Sinai by three, highly efficient, if slightly nauseated. I found Mom and Greg sitting side by side in the waiting room, eating sandwiches, which I was relieved to see were not cheese. The tests had run long, and Goldstein had treated them to tuna fish from the cafeteria. Mom seemed content. As Greg filled me in on what I'd missed, she laid down her sandwich, looking for a napkin. He reached over, took her hand as he would Dylan's, and wiped her fingers one by one, still speaking, his eyes on my face. When he finished her first hand, he cleaned the other one.

I would never have done that. I would have assumed it to be a violation of both her autonomy and her role as my mother. If there was finger-wiping to be done, she'd be the one to do it, as she would be the first to tell you. Greg's matter-of-fact manner was gentle and loving; it was her docile acceptance that froze me in place. I waited for her to snatch back her hand and say, "Go 'way!" But she didn't.

This was Mom, yet it was not.

As an image, it was hard to shake. When Goldstein called the following Monday to tell me once again that there was nothing structurally wrong beyond the ever-present scar tissue, and the only alternative was to change the pills yet again, I finally said no. I could not tolerate the state she had been in, burning up in that overcoat, writing that desperate plea in her kitchen. What were we ginning her up for, exactly? What was she supposed to do with that extra energy? None of those pills enabled her to read. Or even to follow an episode of *Law & Order*.

In early September she had told me, "The fact that I get up in the morning discourages me. I don't recognize myself in the mirror. I look like a hag." Naturally, I was alarmed. What could I do to improve things for her? I asked. How could I make her happier? "You can't make me happier," she said curtly. "I'm losing myself. What's to be happy about?"

That was the conversation that prompted me to agree when Goldstein wanted to introduce an additional antidepressant. And made me insist we implement his prescription of pushing her out into the world, to participate. I enrolled her in a post-stroke exercise class at Burke, a rehab facility, three times a week. She took her ceramics class every week and attended Connections, the twice-a-month lecture series at the Jewish Community Center. She and Caroline visited the library regularly, because it was familiar and Mom liked being there.

But past that, she shut down. She now refused to even visit the Metropolitan Museum of Art or the Bronx Botanical Gardens, which had always been among her favorite places. She wanted to stay home. She wanted to feel safe. She wanted, truth be told, to be left alone.

The fear of losing control had always stalked her, specifically the fear of losing her mind. "Pull the plug, don't let me live like that," she begged us, over and over, long before dementia set in, almost as if she expected it. Her fear was so specific and consistent, I can't help but think that in some ways it was the life she had secretly flirted with—there but not there, impervious to accomplishment. For decades, she had been beautiful and brilliant and hardworking and dogged. She had to buy two pairs of shoes in order to get one, do twice what any of her contemporaries did to feel okay. She didn't have two children, she had four. She wasn't just a housewife, she was a professor. She wasn't just a professor, she was an administrator. Unless she was busy every minute of every day, she wasn't doing her best. Keeping up that kind of control breeds an exhaustion that ultimately begs for release.

As for the physiological changes in her life, she had decided she didn't want to be a good sport. She was enraged, and she had every right to be. So when it came to adapting, she had a bad attitude. She wanted out, and that included out of my Girl Scout, can-do, take-charge approach to life, to her life. Yes, I had been trying to make her better. When I couldn't achieve that, I tried to create a new better. She didn't want that one, either.

Ultimately, she chose acceptance. After she had fought it and I had fought it and we'd logged all those hours with doctors and hospitals and cried our way through boxes of Kleenex and said all the right things, in between saying all the wrong things, she was the one who moved toward it, not me. So I had to stop and ask: Who was I doing this for? Which one of us was I trying to save?

Two weeks after the Sinai visit, I sat down with Mom again to see how she was feeling about things.

"In each part of life you do what you have to do," she said.

So what was she doing in this part?

"Dying."

I met her eye. "What does that feel like?"

"Slowing down, not as engaged in things as I used to be. I don't give a shit about a lot of stuff, and that's a good part."

I was surprised that she swore; that was unlike her. "You believe in life after death, though, right?"

"Me?"

"Yes, you. When I was growing up, you told me that I shouldn't be afraid to die because when I did, you would be there waiting for me. So I've never been afraid to die."

"I take it back."

"What?"

She shrugged. "If you want me to believe it, I'll believe it. I'm too rational a person to believe it."

"Don't you want to see your parents?"

"Not my mother. She was horrendous. Beautiful, but also stupid, which is one thing I could never forgive her for. She used to make fun of me reading books." She folded her arms, as if still protecting herself. "I didn't talk back to my mother. I should have."

Her changing her stance on the afterlife genuinely surprised me. As a rule, Jews don't believe in the afterlife, a notion I find sorely lacking in imagination. That she and I had the idea of one in common not only comforted me, but interested me. Could she just have been placating me all those years?

Maybe. But.

Even if she had forgotten it now, I could still see her flushed face beneath that tree at camp as she recounted her showdown with God. "I love you," she'd cried, even when she'd meant to cry "I hate you." Whatever happened there had confounded us both, but propelled her inexorably forward. I couldn't help but wonder if something like that might happen again.

Goldstein and I agreed to keep one antidepressant and to add an antianxiety pill. That sounded like a good idea for me, too. It seemed almost everyone I knew was taking those—Xanax, or something like it. Maybe, instead of depending on a few drinks each night to get to sleep, I could take something. Imagine waking up every morning without an impending sense of doom. Imagine not waking up in the middle of most nights, panic-stricken, picturing Mom going downstairs in her nightgown, out through the lobby when the doorman was on break, and into oncoming traffic.

My doctor prescribed a low dosage of Effexor. I took the first pill around midnight, before I went to sleep. I awoke at two-thirty a.m., mouth dry, heart pounding. What the hell was going on? It was like an anxiety attack on steroids. By five o'clock I still wasn't asleep, though I started to dream. *This is a hallucination,* I thought. *Sleep!* I couldn't. At nine, I called the doctor, hysterical. She told me not to take any more and sent over three Xanax instead. They sat in my medicine cabinet for a year—just in case—before I threw them out.

Back to the kitchen, my tranquilizer of choice. But I couldn't think of what to cook that would make me feel better. I missed Nat and Simon. Though Frank and I saw them frequently, they were in their twenties and no longer in residence each weekend, gobbling up the two pounds of spaghetti with pesto I used to keep just for their snacks. They were champion eaters, those kids.

I found a recipe I used to make them, keema curry. It was quick and easy and came from, of all places, Rick Rodgers's *365 Ways to Cook Hamburger and Other Ground Meats.* This was a book I liked to read when I was depressed, maybe because it was an entire collection of chopped-meat variations. Even though many of the recipes didn't appeal to me, a chapter like "Around the World in 21 Meatballs," which encompassed everything from Swedish meatballs to chicken chow mein meatballs, returned me to the glory days of chicken Polynesian. The only dishes I had actually ever made from the book were the keema curry, or No. 206, "Indian Ground Beef and Pea Sauté" as the book called it, and No. 143, "Easy Baked Ziti," which was easy as advertised and also delicious. It never occurred to me to use any of its recipes for spaghetti and meat sauce; Mom's version was the gold standard, even though it lacked the dimensions of a classic Bolognese containing pork and milk. Still, there was a pronounced alchemy between ingredients like Del Monte tomato sauce, garlic powder, and dried basil that could not be underestimated. At least not by me.

Given that it was summer and not exactly meat sauce season, I decided to make the keema again, but in a fit of puritanical idiocy substituted ground turkey since it was healthier and it was only Frank and me eating it. I suppose it is not surprising that I am a rotten improviser in the kitchen. I have always had to follow a recipe as written, repeatedly, before attempting to alter it to my own taste. This version was completely awful, like eating curried erasers. So the antidepressant hadn't worked for me, and neither had the psychic tranquilizer. Just like Mom.

As Thanksgiving neared, however, Mom did grow calmer. I did not. I spoke with Roberta Epstein about the possibility of another family meeting. I filled her in on what was happening with Mom, how she was there, but not there.

"It's called ambiguous loss," she told me. "Gone, but not gone. She is your mother, but not the mother you knew. If she had died, it would be easier to grieve the loss. It's hard to do that when she's sitting in front of you. That person is no longer the person you knew."

But she was! At least sometimes. Though to be honest, that was occurring less and less. Still, when she was in there, it meant everything to me to see her. When Frank's mother died, her death was sudden—violent and traumatizing. Frank had spoken to her on the phone for an hour the night before the car crash. He adored her. To have her disappear without warning, without a chance to say good-bye, tore him apart. He feels the brutality of the loss to this day. But would it have been better if she'd lived long enough to be like my mother, there but not there? She was sixty-four when she died, and in perfect health. Would he have wanted to watch her ebb away before his eyes? Of course he would. He would give up almost anything to have the chance to see her as herself again, even fleetingly.

Would I want my mother to be taken from me in an instant, without warning? I used to think the answer was no. But as hard as that would be on me, maybe it would have been better for her. To die as herself. Because the worst part of her situation was watching her know that she wasn't *in* there anymore—watching her face as she heard herself speak and saw how other people reacted. That was cruelty beyond measure. I told Roberta that if I could see Mom and appreciate her when she appeared, no matter how briefly, maybe that would encourage her to come back. But in my heart I knew it didn't work that way.

I remembered how Mom had taken care of Uncle Selig in the years before he died in 1984. His wife had predeceased him, and they'd had no children. He lived alone in the city, and Mom became his personal Meals on Wheels, making brisket and roast chicken and packaging them in individual portions so he would have something to heat up every night of the week.

Like the rest of the family, Selig was an avid eater. (He once dubbed a photograph of Great-Grandma Tessie, Grandma, and his other sister, Sarah—three hefty gals—"The Beef Trust.") I recall being with him at a relative's apartment for lunch in the early eighties on the Upper East Side of Manhattan. It was a lovely spread, as they say, including the then trendy chicken salad with pecans and grapes. Selig sat next to me in the living room, setting his plate down on the coffee table. "What is this?" he asked me, indicating the chicken salad. I enumerated the ingredients, but they didn't seem to register. "It's lunch," I said assertively. He gazed sadly at the plate. "This isn't lunch," he said. "Brisket is lunch."

Like Grandma and Sarah—and Mom, for that matter—Selig developed what they used to call midlife-onset diabetes, now Type 2, along with a form of dementia that centered on paranoia. He was convinced that someone was after him, although he didn't know who. The Man, as we named his illusory enemy, became an important figure in Selig's life, and he couldn't be talked out of believing in him no matter how hard Mom argued otherwise. When I was going through her safety deposit box, looking for some legal document, I found a letter to her written in Selig's meticulous handwriting, on lined yellow paper.

Dear Bobby,

That thief was here again while I was gone for an hour or so, and took my address book from the desk. I guess there was nothing more important for him to take at this time.

I want to caution you and your family IN CASE he makes contact and spreads false rumors and/or other information, to disregard anything he might say or want you to do.

Check with me first under any circumstance because I don't intend to ask any stranger to convey messages for me. I would go to the Police Department for that. I know he would follow me and then call you (or someone else) when I am not at home for you to check immediately—so you bide your time.

I believe he is after some clues in the address book relating to bankers, vault numbers, bonds, and other valuables that he might secure through chicanaree.

So please be on your guard. Call me when you get a moment.

Love,
Selig

Mom's loving uncle was still loving. Could you say he was the same person she had always adored? Not exactly, but so what? Part of what defines a person is who they are to *you*. As long as you're still there, so are they. Gone but not gone was ambiguous, but love wasn't. It might be the only reliable way to define someone you love: who they are to you. That's why it's difficult to see a parent in any other role.

Along with Selig's letter in the safety deposit box, I found a note to Mom from my former editor at the *Times*, John Montorio.

It was dated in the late 1990s, after the three of us had lunch together in the city. It didn't say much, just that he was glad to have met her after hearing so much about her. And he made some reference to her being a woman of mystery.

As I recall that lunch, she was being a woman of reticence, as usual. She was never one to open up to a stranger, not even one preapproved by me. I have a vague memory of him teasing her about that at the time. But what struck me was that she had kept the letter. In her safety deposit box, with birth certificates and stock certificates. She apparently valued being thought of as mysterious, and I found that mysterious, because in my definition of my mother, she doesn't think of things like that. Perhaps she liked someone finding her secrets alluring, because she had always found them shameful.

So who exactly was my mother? At that point, she was a seventy-seven-year-old woman who could no longer remember how many years she had been married or any of her children's birthdays. She did not recognize her grandchildren. She stood in my apartment, where she had visited me for nineteen years, and asked me who lived there. She could not remember that her younger daughter had cancer. But the fierce, loving, prickly person she had always been was still in there, fleetingly for sure, and I didn't want to let her go. I wanted to track her down and keep her there.

But now I had to face the truth. She didn't want to be tracked down. She didn't want to be kept, anywhere. "Is someone here for me?" she'd asked the doorman. "Am I moving?" she asked Kiki.

She was sensing it was time to go. Even halfway out of her mind, she seemed to recognize the truth of that. When I still couldn't.

Toward the end of the summer, as we stood out in her garden, she'd said, "It's not like my old garden. I don't work here much. It's not in the front of my mind." I said nothing. We had actually worked on it quite a bit just a few weeks before.

Then she told me she planned to move into Selig's apartment. He had left it to her when he died, and she still owned it. I thought it best not to remind her that Greg lived there with his family.

I walked her upstairs and offered to tuck her in for her nap. "I'm not sleeping, I have things to do," she proclaimed. I hoped that didn't mean making three dinners, but again I said nothing. Once outside the building, I looked up at her apartment and there she was, standing on the terrace, waving. I felt buoyed by that. Often, no matter how long we had been together, she didn't remember I'd been there, even a minute after I'd gone.

I love you, she mouthed. I blew her kisses and patted my heart and mouthed back, *I love you*. She was wearing a yellow shirt and she was smiling and her blond hair shone in the sunlight. She was so beautiful and she beamed down on me with so much love and I waved and she waved. And then her expression changed—ever so slightly—as she looked at me standing there waving, and she grew impatient, possibly a shade scornful, as if to say, "Enough already."

Out of the blue, I thought of Hickory Hill, a summer camp at a country club where she had been a counselor when I was three or four. We were near the pool, and she had given me a dime to buy potato chips at the snack bar. I waited for her to take my hand and lead me there, but she shook her head. She wasn't going with me. I was a big girl, and she wanted me to get in line alone. It's okay, she told me. I'll be right here, watching.

I wanted no part of that experiment and was about to throw a fit, but there was something in her face—the same something I had glimpsed just now—that assured me I had no choice. I was a big girl, whether I wanted to be or not. I got in line.

And that day, as I watched her on the terrace, it was she who made the decision again. I stopped waving and smiling and patting my heart. I left.

Spaghetti and Meat Sauce

....

⅓ cup canola oil
2 medium onions, minced
1 ½ pounds ground chuck
1 ½ pounds ground veal
Salt and pepper
3 ½ teaspoons garlic powder
3 teaspoons dried oregano
3 teaspoons dried basil
1 (32-ounce) jar Classico Tomato & Basil sauce
1 (8-ounce) can Del Monte tomato sauce
1 (6-ounce) can tomato paste
2 pounds dried spaghetti

In a large skillet, heat the oil. Add the onions and cook on medium heat until soft, 5 to 7 minutes. Add the meat to the pan, breaking it up and mixing it with the onions. Liberally salt the meat mixture and add pepper to taste. Cook until it loses the raw color, about 10 minutes more.

Add the spices and mix thoroughly. Add the Classico sauce, the Del Monte sauce, and the tomato paste, and combine with the meat. Cover and cook at a low simmer, stirring periodically, for 30 minutes. Taste and adjust seasonings. Turn off the heat and let it sit for 30 to 60 minutes.

Return the sauce to the heat and let simmer while you make the spaghetti. Bring a large pot of water to a boil and salt liberally. Add the spaghetti and cook until tender. Drain and serve with the sauce.

Serves 6

Eight

. . . . ● . . . . .

One day the following winter, a doorman in my apartment building presented me with what seemed to be a body wrapped in garbage bags. On closer inspection, it turned out to be Mom's mink coat. When I was growing up, her mink was a light brown number, with bracelet sleeves and a deep collar—very Rat Pack. After thirty years of wear had rendered it more rat than pack, she'd gotten this black one, simple and classic.

I did not own fur myself. Neither did Phoebe. She did not want the coat; she was too tall for it anyway. I did not want it, but I didn't want my father giving it away now that Mom didn't wear it anymore. I knew I was supposed to put it in storage during the summer, then wear it once or twice each winter to some big event, as Mom had. That coat meant so much to her—some finish line she had crossed, victorious.

In 2000, just before her strokes started, Frank and I had taken her and Dad to a French restaurant in the city. It was Christmas week, and we thought it would be a fun, festive thing to do. Frank and I arrived at the restaurant to find Mom in her mink, refusing to check it. Not only that, she refused to take it off. She had heard stories about women dumb enough to check a mink in a New York City restaurant only to have it stolen. (Why, then, had she worn it to a New York City restaurant?) She and I were seated on a banquette, and everyone else in the room was either staring or trying not to. Finally, I insisted she let it off her shoulders. She'd still be sitting on it, after all. If a thief dared try to lift her up during the meal, she could apprehend him single-handedly.

This obsessive behavior was nothing new with Mom. She was like this with her few pieces of good jewelry, too. She kept them in her safety deposit box, so when she wanted to wear something she had to drive to the bank and sign her name and present her key. The next day she took it right back as if the jewelry didn't really belong to her. She and Dad were both so used to not having, so used to yearning, that neither of them had ever gotten the hang of deserving.

Frank and I once traveled with them to attend a family wedding in Philadelphia, when Mom was still Mom. The four of us met at Penn Station to take the train together on Saturday afternoon. Dad wouldn't shake hands with Frank or kiss me because he was sick, he said. He had a stomachache or a virus or a cold. Mom was pleasant, but subdued. The wedding wasn't until Sunday, and Frank and I were treating them to a night at the Four Seasons, a splurge made palatable to me, the heir apparent to yearning and not deserving, by a substantially discounted weekend rate. Our plan for dinner was to try Le Bec-Fin, Philadelphia's famously old-school fancy French restaurant. Dad had been obsessed with it for years, but of course had never been.

Once ensconced at the hotel, I asked Dad to explore with me before dinner, in tribute to our Jewish War Veterans tradition. We walked through the stately lobby, sadly devoid of pinball machines, surveyed the dark bar, then took the elevator to the indoor swimming pool. As we walked through the elaborately tiled area, enveloped by the familiar steamy smell of chlorine, he seemed almost abashed. "Pretty swifty," he said. When I agreed, he mumbled something about not being used to a place like this. I turned to look at him, genuinely surprised. To me, this hotel was no more elegant, no more "swifty," than the ones we'd stayed at in the Catskills.

At Le Bec-Fin, the surroundings were almost laughably elaborate, as was the attire of the clientele. I'd never seen so many prom dresses out of prom season on young and old alike. Mom had gone from subdued to actively irritated; she'd never been much for ostentation. But as course after course of delicious food was served, accompanied by glass after glass of good wine, she relaxed, and her face glowed in the candlelight. Dad was talking and laughing and eating everything in sight. Whatever illness he thought he'd had earlier in the day had apparently disappeared. During the final hour of the meal, my parents were as relaxed and happy as I had ever seen them—the people I had always wished them to be.

For weeks after that trip, Dad called anyone he knew who

spoke French, trying to get a consensus on the proper pronunciation of "Le Bec-Fin." He was convinced Frank and I had it wrong, and insisted on unearthing the truth. It wasn't enough to have enjoyed it; he now had to dissect it. Mom had taken a jar of candies from her room as a souvenir and kept it prominently displayed on her dresser at home (it had been part of the minibar, we discovered when paying the bill, but never told her). She rhapsodized about the plush towels at the Four Seasons, comparing them with the ones she and Dad used at the last Jewish War Veterans convention they attended in the Catskills. They were so thin, she told me, you could hold them up to the light and see through them. I wasn't sure what upset me more, the image of those threadbare towels in use forty years after they were plush, or the two of them returning year after year to use them.

But after this wondrous weekend, neither ever said, "Hey, Philadelphia was so much fun, let's do it again!" Or, "Philadelphia was so much fun, let's pick another place to go together!" (When I said that to them, there was no response past a watery "We'll see.") They had both worked so hard to get through it—grappling with luxury they felt they hadn't earned, and the anxiety that roiled in each of them—that once the memory, the story of it, was set, it could never be improved. They were back to the stomach virus and the safety deposit box, safe and sound.

As a kid, of course, I'd never figured this out. Listening to my parents, Kiki, Aunt Marcia, and Uncle Bernie talk about the world, I'd believed they were seasoned travelers, full of funny stories and informed opinions. And I was right about the stories and opinions—as far as they went. But as I grew up, I realized that this Algonquin Round Table was composed of a college professor, a public relations executive, a secretary, a bookkeeper, and a pharmacist, all of whom worked hard and traveled some, but were hardly jet-setters. Still, I thought that given half the chance, my parents would jump to do more.

Having been raised by fearful people, I naturally wanted to be just like them, for company, if nothing else. But I wasn't. I actually did want to leave the house, at least sometimes. Whatever fears I had of the unknown did not stop me from wanting to explore. For Mom, exploration was fraught with danger, both literal and figurative. For all her love of learning—the flights of fancy she allowed her mind—fear protected her, kept her in her seat, where she couldn't fall down. Instead, she'd pushed me out the door with a head full of bromides and directives to conquer at all costs. As if my achievements could vaporize her fears and connect her to the world.

Years before our Philly trip, soon after we were married, I'd accompanied Frank to Ireland, where he was reviewing plays in Dublin while still a drama critic for the *Times*. I called Mom and Dad from an inn we stayed at outside the city, enchanted to find that at eleven o'clock on a summer's night, it was still light outside. Mom's response to this revelation seemed distinctly tepid; I got the feeling she would have preferred to have seen it herself. With me.

When Dad got on the phone, he sounded elated by this news. I knew he would tell everyone he saw the next day that his daughter had called from Ireland in broad daylight at eleven o'clock at night. And I knew he would consider it his great good fortune that he could hear about it and talk about it without ever having to go there himself.

After letting the coat stay in the front hall for a few days, I unwrapped it and was surprised to discover that it smelled like Mom. It was soft and shiny and felt wonderful. I hung it in the front hall closet and started visiting it. I couldn't tell if it depressed me or made me glad.

Then I thought I might wear it. Break the spell, enjoy it in a way my mother never could. Frank was asked to be a presenter at the Theater Hall of Fame Awards on a freezing night in late January, and the event was black-tie. "Mink is warm and light," I remember Mom saying. And of course she was right. It was delightful in every way, until I arrived at the Gershwin Theatre. I took an uneasy look at the coat check line and kept walking. What if I got cold during the ceremony? I took my seat on one of the folding chairs set up in the lobby, where the event took place, the coat bundled on my lap. The program began. I crossed my legs. A sleeve slipped out. I gathered it back. The other sleeve slipped out. I gathered it back. When it was time to applaud a speaker and there was commotion, I tried folding it inside out to get some traction on it. The woman next to me pulled her skirt in, annoyed. My evening bag slid to the floor. I left it there, my arms encircling this mass on my lap as if it were alive.

A reception followed at the Friars Club. Frank steered me into the coat check line with a look on his face that was not to be argued with.

At the end of the evening, I went to retrieve the coat. Because there were so many people, they had moved the racks upstairs to a large banquet room. The coat check woman was apologetic. In the move, some of the hangers had lost their numbers. Did I recognize my coat?

I felt my throat close. One night out and I'd done what Mom had successfully guarded against in forty years of mink coat ownership: I'd lost it. I looked at the sea of black garments before me, the scrap of pink paper with the check number on it damp in my hand. I stomped up and down, back and forth. Okay, there! I found it, the coat glossy on the hanger with my black pashmina scarf looped around it. I looked at the coat behind it, a black mink glossy on the hanger with a black pashmina looped around it. I pawed at the first one. Aha! *BMW*, Mom's initials, on the lining. I pulled it on, barely feeling my fingertips, my adrenaline was pumping so hard. Do I need to say that was the last time that coat left the closet? It took me two years to work up the nerve to even put it into storage.

I did not share my adventures in mink with Mom. Even though she would forget the story soon enough, I did not want to agitate her. Since Goldstein had added the antianxiety drug and he and I agreed to stop changing her medication further, she had been on a more even keel, and I wanted to keep it that way. While her illness was not progressive in the way of Alzheimer's, it was progressive in its own way.

We were sitting at the table one day having tea, and I mentioned Caroline. Mom frowned, as if struggling to remember something. "How is she related to me?" she asked.

Talk then turned to a recent birthday party for Ilan, which we had both attended. "Do you remember it?" I asked.

"No," she said steadily. "I'm telling you the truth. I'm terribly sorry, I just can't remember." She looked at me. "Did I give him something?"

"Yes, clothes." My father had bought them.

"Well," she said, "at least I did that."

Still, there was an occasional glimpse of her. When I took notes during our time together, she would ask why. At first I told her I wanted to make sure I remembered everything she said, which was true. When I decided to write a book about her, I told her that. Having spent much of her life watching students take notes as she spoke, she was comfortable with it. One day, I brought sandwiches from Junior's in Grand Central Terminal for lunch. They came in plastic containers, and once I had opened them, I couldn't get them closed. As I tussled with one, she reached over and snapped it shut. I laughed at yet another demonstration of my lack of manual dexterity. "I am a spaz," I said, "and you are not." She nodded toward my pen. "Write that down, too."

During our next visit to Goldstein, I asked him about the oblong bulge I'd noticed on Mom's stomach whenever I helped her undress. She would ask, "What is this?" pointing to the thin purple scar that ran down it vertically. I'd tell her it was the legacy of the aortobifemoral bypass. "That happened to me?" she would ask, amazed. "It did," I assured her. "It's why your feet are warm for the first time in your life."

Goldstein said the bulge was an abdominal hernia, itself a legacy of the bypass surgery. The stomach muscles were too weak to hold. We went back to the surgeon, who recommended it be fixed; if the intestine got stuck in the opening, it could become infected. That didn't sound good. She sent us to another surgeon who specialized in hernias. He said Mom would have to be hospitalized for three or four days. She would have some pain, but he would insert a piece of mesh that would keep the intestine contained.

That sounded reasonable to me. It was late June and I was about to spend a week in Los Angeles reporting a story for the *Times Magazine*, so I scheduled the surgery for early July. The day before I left, I heard from Dr. Novich, Mom's internist in the suburbs, who would do the pre-op tests. He was an older man, a laidback, voice-of-experience general practitioner, a welcome antidote to Goldstein's cutting-edge medical school mojo.

"Is this surgery necessary?" he asked. I was taken aback. Well, I thought it was, based on two surgeons' recommending it. Novich kept questioning me. What were the actual chances of the hernia becoming a problem? I didn't know. Had anyone discussed the effects of anesthesia on someone with Mom's level of dementia? She would be in a strange place, in pain, disoriented. Had anyone thought of that?

By the time I hung up, I was shaken. All these years, I had made decisions about her care like clockwork. But now I stopped. Was stopped. He was right to ask those questions. Why hadn't I?

I looked at my notes. Laparoscopic ventral hernia repair with mesh, to prevent her intestine from getting stuck in the opening. But I hadn't asked how likely it was that that would happen. I had just assumed it would.

From L.A., I called the hernia surgeon. He could have run for political office, the way he didn't answer my question. The chance of the hernia becoming an emergency was small, he finally acknowledged. How small? Ten percent? Less? He couldn't really say—but probably, yes.

Not sure what to do, I e-mailed my siblings, filling them in on Novich's reservations. I could have just called the surgeon back, postponed the surgery, gotten another opinion. But by that point, I felt so defeated, so wrong. I felt suddenly incapable of making a decision. Everyone had stopped asking me when Mommy was getting better because they finally figured out that Mommy wasn't going to get better. Maybe the choices I made were wrong. Maybe someone else knew something I didn't.

I reconsidered the need for surgery, and Emmett agreed with me, hoping to minimize trauma—mental, physical, and emotional. Phoebe and Greg disagreed, advocating surgery on the grounds of "better safe than sorry." I called another doctor, a friend, for advice. "What you're telling me," he said, "is there's an eight percent chance of a problem. In other words, there is a ninety-two percent chance that everything will be fine. Do you put her through pain and disorientation and possible complications if there's a ninety-two percent chance of everything being fine?"

No. That was my answer, and I was sticking to it. Or thought I was. The e-mails continued for the full week I was in L.A. without resolution. I called my father to ask his opinion. "Leave it alone," he said. I called Caroline to ask hers. "I think it would be hard for her," she said. I called Goldstein, who recommended another surgeon for another opinion. I scheduled an appointment a month later.

In the meantime, I was losing my bearings. Before I left for L.A., I had gone to Scarsdale to take Mom out to lunch. She was in a rare spiral of agitation at the time; she asked Dad repeatedly what she should make for me. When I arrived, I found a note he had left her: *Alex coming to lunch. She will do it ALL.*

I had reached my limit of doing it all. What if I made a terrible mistake? What if she had the surgery and something went wrong? What if she didn't have the surgery and something went wrong? *My fault, my fault, my fault.* It was like a drumbeat in my head that wouldn't stop.

At the end of July, I was scheduled to fly to London for the magazine to write about a celebrity who was in production on a movie. It would be a quick trip, two nights and back. In the years since Mom had been ill, my work had turned into a refuge from doctors and hospitals; asking questions on just about any topic other than dementia was like a mini-vacation. Having interviewed people for decades, I actually felt like I knew what I was doing, which was another relief. Though I couldn't write as frequently, each piece provided welcome respite.

Interviewing is its own skill set, one I learned quickly. Early on I realized it is a mistake to allow a publicist or friend to sit in during the process; the subject ends up speaking to them, not me, in their own intimate shorthand, revealing nothing. The most important part of interviewing, next to extensive preparation, is listening. Very few people are capable of listening in real life, but for a journalist, it's critical. So many profiles end up being about the writer, not the subject, because the writer was too self-involved to hear someone else. After I wrote a profile on Helen Gurley Brown, the founding editor of *Cosmopolitan*, she told me that I "listened maniacally." It takes one to know one, certainly, and it remains one of my favorite compliments.

I also learned early to sit down with a subject before talking to other people about them. I want to form my own impressions without letting them be colored by someone else's affinity or enmity. When Simon was in grade school, he had an art teacher who told the class, "Paint what you see, not what you know." I considered that excellent advice. "Write what you see, not what you know" is the rule I follow to avoid preconception and to respond to the truth as it unfolds. That said, a profile is completely subjective. The writer gets all sorts of personal information and makes a thousand choices about how to use it. You can love your subjects or hate them. Or forget them the minute you're done.

Most interviews are straightforward. You ask, they answer. Sometimes you get a curveball. I interviewed the musical theater diva Elaine Stritch over dinner at Tout Va Bien, an old-time French bistro in the theater district. The place was packed, and she was chatting away on the banquette as I took notes. Suddenly, she stopped. "Forgot my shot," she said, pulling a hypodermic filled with insulin from her purse. I thought she might just lift her sleeve, but that wouldn't have been show business. She raised herself onto her knees, pulled her blouse from her pants, and gathered it up, up—every eye in the place was on her at that point—before plunging the needle into her completely bared abdomen. Bon appétit!

I spent a weekend interviewing Don Rickles at the MGM Grand in Las Vegas. His acid comic persona aside, Rickles is famously a sweetheart offstage, and he was a great interview— open, unguarded, thoughtful. He talked about the toll it took being on the road so much when his children were younger. In later years when they got him on the phone at home, they'd ask, "Where's Mom?" He said he wished they would call sometimes and ask, "Where's Dad?" He sort of winced when he said it, and that moment of sadness, of exclusion, was haunting.

In the almost twenty years since then, celebrity interviews have changed enormously. There are more layers of people— agents, managers, publicists, producers—so arranging an interview can now take weeks instead of days. In that endlessly torpid July of 2009, I found myself playing phone and e-mail tag with both an American team of representatives and a British team for the celebrity on the movie set, with no plan in sight. An on-set visit? Absolutely. Until the next day when it was out of the question.

To prepare for the interview, or not to prepare, that was my question. In many ways, writing a piece is like cooking a meal. I can spend days, weeks, or months reporting a column or profile that someone reads in just minutes. Or doesn't. I once saw a man on the subway start a piece I had written in the paper and, after a paragraph or two, turn the page. Those moments keep you humble.

Under normal circumstances—meaning when I was sane—I would have pulled the plug on this piece immediately. So many layers of incompetent people was an unmistakable red flag. But nothing seemed normal anymore, and I'd lost my compass. *Maybe I shouldn't do what I always do,* I thought. *Instead of being so definitive, maybe I should give them all a chance, see what happens next.* I reserved the hotel. I booked the flights. I prepared and prepared and prepared.

During this time, the issue of Mom's surgery still hung in abeyance, our appointment with the third surgeon a few weeks away. I woke up nightly at four a.m., falling back to sleep only sometimes. Even my 5:15 bus on Riverside Drive didn't do the trick anymore.

I was unraveling. Ten days before I was due to go to London, I woke up and started to weep. I got on the train to go see Mom, still weeping. I got to Mom's apartment, where I sat with her and Caroline and wept some more. Overtired, I said. Too much work. Caroline kissed Mom good-bye, and Mom and I walked over to the diner for lunch. I stopped weeping only long enough to order.

"Why are you so tired?" Mom asked. "Are you worried about everything?"

"Yes," I said. "I feel bad if you have to have an operation."

"What is it, a big deal?"

"Maybe just to me. You have a hernia. It's that bulge in your stomach."

She shrugged. "I have to be perfect when I die? Why is that?"

I didn't answer.

"What's the big deal with this operation?" she asked.

"They put mesh in your abdomen to keep your bowel in place."

"Very good, it should know its place."

"I just don't want you to be in pain." This brought a fresh wave of tears.

She shook her head. "So what do I have to do? Just show up, take anesthesia, and heal? Sounds good to me. Don't cry."

"What if you're in pain for a week?"

"I'll take pills."

She was so game, she wanted so much to make me happy, be a good girl, do everything right. It broke my heart.

She watched me cry. "You feel sorry about yourself," she said.

I nodded. That was it, exactly.

A few days later, I got a message from the celebrity's publicists telescoping the two-day trip to a one-hour chat on my way back to the airport. For a cover story. I called my editor, who agreed with me: Game over. I had worked for a month preparing for nothing. It seemed of a piece with everything else.

Finally, Mom and I had our appointment with the third surgeon. "The chances of the hernia rupturing are extremely small," he said. "This is gestalt, instead of science, but based on the exam, my gestalt is that it is a fairly unlikely event that this will either become an emergency or bother you." He also noted that Mom already had foreign matter in the abdomen—the prosthetic veins from the aortobifemoral bypass—and to introduce still another material, mesh, was to invite infection. "It's a low incidence, but it has disaster potential," he said. "If this doesn't bother you, you don't bother it."

He was so kind and clear and smart, I thought I might start blubbering again. When he left the examining room, Mom looked down on me somberly from the table. "You are really getting gray," she said. I burst out laughing. When we were back on the street, walking toward Caroline's car, Mom pointed wordlessly to a license plate. "GEVALT," it read. And then some.

Goldstein thought this surgeon's information and judgment were both sound. I e-mailed my siblings and each agreed about skipping the surgery. We had exhausted ourselves on the topic by then. I had exhausted myself as well. In the midst of all this care-giving and caretaking—caring, caring everywhere, with no respite in sight—I had to admit I was more than a little enraged. At Mom. Yes.

Why hadn't she taken better care of herself? How could she have gotten to this point? It was actually quite convenient of her to decide *now* that she didn't believe in an afterlife. Because once we were both in it and I could get hold of her as herself again, I would happily *kill* her with my bare hands. Why hadn't she gone back to get her carotid arteries checked when she was supposed to? Why did she wait until she lost so much oxygen to her brain? Why hadn't she taken medication to prevent strokes if her own mother had had them? Why did she smoke too much and eat too much and never exercise? Why? Why? Why?

I knew that none of that necessarily mattered. Grandma never smoked, and she'd had the same kind of strokes Mom had. We all know someone whose ninety-five-year-old father smoked two packs a day until he died of old age. These things are arbitrary. It's why, having written two novels, I've come to realize that truth-telling, so exacting, so bald, is hard to beat. If you look at the actual events of life, the tiny individual stories, you see actions that confound both logic and imagination. When you write fiction, an editor says no, life is not like that. You must add this, subtract that. You need a balance. But life often lacks balance. It is random and painful and disorienting. Or deliberate and joyous and reassuring. But never in equal measure.

Two years earlier, I had been approached to write an article for the *Times Magazine* about the movie *The Savages*, in which Philip Seymour Hoffman and Laura Linney play siblings whose long-absent father loses his marbles and becomes their unwanted responsibility. They move him to a home and voilà! Within a few months he's dead. Like magic. Everyone gets a big dramatic scene—For Your Consideration this awards season—before moving on. Just like life! No, thank you, I told them. The Hollywood version came too late for me.

In 2007, I interviewed Christine Ebersole before she won a Tony Award for her remarkable performance as Edie Beale in the Broadway musical *Grey Gardens*. She revealed that her own mother had been suffering from memory loss, and was living with her and her husband and their three children. Wow, I said. You're performing eight shows a week while raising three kids under twelve, and you've got your mom living with you, too? And she answered, "It's a privilege." She talked about it being her turn to give the care now, and as she spoke, what knocked me out was her acceptance. She wasn't trying to fix it, she wasn't storming the halls of Mount Sinai hunting for another doctor, another test that would provide the aha moment when the reason, the secret, would be ultimately revealed. Her mom couldn't take care of herself, so she was taking care of her. That's all.

It took three more years before I could accept even a small part of my mother's condition without considering it my personal failure or betrayal. I had tried going online to *The New Old Age*, the *Times*'s blog about caring for elderly parents, to look for some virtual company among children of dementia patients. But I was put off by the many comments that devolved into petty sniping about what other people could or could not afford in time, money, or effort. Everyone who loves someone with dementia is suffering. To rate the suffering seemed beside the point to me. In that system the only way you were truly a good daughter was to give up your job, trash your marriage, and become your parent's caretaker twenty-four hours a day in your own home, with no one to help you. Maybe there are parents who would applaud a child's doing that, but I knew my mother would have been grievously disappointed to see me toss aside the life she had so painstakingly raised me to lead.

"Is someone here for me?" Mom had asked. She was leaving,

she was dying—and she was still here, doing just fine, by the way, from the neck down. No big dramatic scenes. No third-act resolution. No awards for bravery for keeping going while realizing how diminished you are, watching flashes of yourself crackle then disappear, like lightning.

That is what had been tormenting me: She knew something was wrong, she tried by sheer acts of will to overcome it and could not. I tried doing the same and I could not. I never wanted her to think I'd abandoned her. I never wanted her to be alone. I wanted her to know I was fighting for her. I kept asking what I could do to help her, what I could do to make her happier. She looked at me pityingly every time. "There's nothing you can do, because it's not up to you," she would say. "You're here with me now. That's enough."

I think back to a holiday celebration at my apartment, when she was already well into her dementia. In the midst of the family chaos, I'd watched her and my father sitting alone at the table. It was at the end of a meal, and unmindful of the din of toddlers jockeying for toys and world supremacy, he was talking, only to her. He was recounting some historic event, in monologue form as is his wont, but she has always been engaged by his grasp of history. She listened and nodded, and their eyes met and they laughed. Whether or not Mom understood what he was saying at that moment, the ritual of that sort of conversation was comforting and familiar. In the midst of the grandchildren whose names she could not remember, in the midst of anxious adult children who circled her with questions she could not answer, there was my father, oblivious to the surrounding hubbub as he had always been, and there she was, his best audience, listening with her heart if not her head. She was so entirely present in that moment that it took my breath away.

The day I was supposed to have gone to London, Phoebe called. Her company had reorganized, and she'd lost her job. There was simply no good news to be had. I kept struggling to regain my center. When I had been working in Los Angeles in June, Frank had come with me and we'd rented a car with a GPS. Every time we took a wrong turn, the machine's voice said, "Redirecting," but I remembered the word as "recalibrating." I desperately needed to recalibrate. I just didn't know how.

Two weeks later, Frank started to cough. I started to panic. First it was a cold. Then it was bronchitis. We took a week's vacation and he was sick for all of it. Labor Day came and went. He took a second round of antibiotics. Still coughing.

One day when he was working at his desk at home, I sat down next to him. I was concerned about him pushing himself too hard, not giving himself a chance to heal. He was concerned about me, too. The psychological pressures of dealing with Mom had been significant. On the days I saw her, I would come back and sob all night. I was perennially distracted, irritable, sad. It was a definite strain between us. He took my hand in his. "I'm waiting for you to come back to me," he said gently.

I felt crushed. Yes, I'd had the unmistakable sensation of being stuck on pause for too long. But I hadn't taken stock of the sheer length of it, the cumulative toll of this ongoing, endless situation.

How long had it been since I'd been able to give my full attention to my husband? Girlfriends seemed a distant memory. On the days I wasn't either seeing Mom or crying, I needed every free second to work.

I held Frank's hand a while longer, leaning against him. When we were first dating, almost twenty years earlier, we had gone to London together. In the wake of his divorce, he told me, his relationship with his sons had intensified and solidified; he had fallen in love with them all over again. One night, in Piccadilly Circus, I think, with the traffic whizzing by from the wrong direction, he took my hand to cross the street, as if I were Nat or Simon. It was as unconscious a gesture as it was loving. Marriage is such a compilation of roles: friends, lovers, helpmates, for starters. But there are times when you're a parent, too. When the nurturing protective love you feel for your children is the best love you can give to your spouse. I thought of him taking my hand to cross the street then; he was doing it again now. I still wasn't sure about making it to the other side.

Soon afterward, I had an unexpected surprise: Sandy, my cocktail-drinking Mormon friend from high school, whom I hadn't seen in at least ten years, was coming to New York for one night. Her son was in college, her daughter was starting her senior year in high school.

She came on a day when Frank was working out of town. She got to my apartment at two-thirty. We sat down at the table to talk, and when Frank walked in the door at midnight, we hadn't moved. The first thing she'd done was to open my fridge looking for grapefruit juice to mix with her vodka. It was as if we had seen each other the day before. I felt something like hope. Some things remain.

When I visited Mom soon after, I told her all about it. She seemed to remember Sandy, and that made me glad. Our conversations were becoming shorter and shorter. She couldn't hold her train of thought long enough to follow through. "You have beautiful eyebrows," she would tell me when she couldn't think what else to say. Sometimes she would compliment my teeth. Sometimes she would call me Pussycat, as she always had. I wondered if that was because she didn't remember my name, but I didn't have the heart to ask.

We sat at the dining room table that afternoon, and I admired a new napkin holder she'd made in her ceramics class. She had recently given me a free-form bowl that I put on my own dining room table. "You decorate my house," I said.

She smiled at me. "You decorate my heart."

I went into the bathroom and tried not to cry, without success. When I came out she saw I was crying and joined right in. We stood in the hallway with our arms around each other and sobbed—big, racking, awful sobs of surrender. With the exception of my summertime meltdown, I never cried in front of her, or tried not to, because I didn't want to upset her. But somehow, as we clung to each other, drowning in defeat, I felt an unexpected tranquillity take hold.

I had tried and tried and tried to fix her, and I had lost. Utterly, unequivocally lost. And she loved me exactly the same as if I had won.

Later, when I left, she walked me to the elevator. "I'm so happy I had you," she said into my ear.

And even though three years have passed and I have seen her as regularly as always, that was the last real conversation we had.

A t the end of October, Frank had to travel for a few days. He had finally kicked the bronchitis, though it had taken seven weeks. I wanted to make a special dinner for him when he came home, and I knew exactly what it would be: chicken with rosemary and garlic. This was the official dish of the Rich boys, created by my friend Philip when I was first married and wasn't sure what Nat and Simon might like. It's boneless chicken breasts sautéed in olive oil with rosemary and garlic. Over the years, the dish evolved so that I cook the chicken slowly, until the meat turns dark brown and the garlic turns black, even though it doesn't taste burnt. You have to wrap your mind around the idea of a leathery chicken breast—think of it as chicken jerky—but the kids and Frank bonded with it early and never let go. We've amassed a cabinet full of hot sauces, and they use all of them on this chicken. I serve it with rice to soak up the garlic-infused oil and Le Sueur peas, which they like, and which, all these years later, still keep me company.

By now this dish has become for the three of them what Mom's meat loaf was to me—their touchstone, their idea of home. I like it fine, but I have never loved it, any more than Mom loved the food she cooked. I always offered to make her my versions of her dishes, and she always said no. "Make me something I don't make myself," she would say. "Something different. Something new."

Once Frank was home, I put a platter of chicken on the table with all the fixings and opened a bottle of wine. I sat down facing him. "Tell me everything that happened today," I said.

And he did.

Chicken with Rosemary and Garlic

. . . . , ...

> 3 cups extra virgin olive oil, approximately
> 12 ounces (about 80 cloves) peeled garlic, minced in a
>   food processor
> 16 halves large boneless, skinless chicken breasts
>   (8–9 pounds)
> About $\frac{1}{3}$ cup dried rosemary
> Hot sauce, for serving (optional)

Place two large skillets over medium heat and add oil to a depth of about ½ inch. Divide the garlic between the two pans and stir until it begins to sizzle. Reduce heat to medium-low and add as many pieces of chicken as will fill each pan snugly without the pieces overlapping.

Sprinkle each piece of chicken with a scant teaspoon of rosemary. Allow them to cook for 5 minutes, then turn and sprinkle again with a scant teaspoon of rosemary. Keep turning the chicken every 3 minutes until the pieces are well browned on both sides. This should take 30 to 40 minutes. When the chicken is done, transfer it to a platter and keep it warm.

Add oil to the pans as necessary and then add the remaining uncooked chicken. Repeat the process, stirring the garlic to keep it from burning (although it will eventually turn dark brown).

When all the chicken is cooked, arrange on a platter and top with the browned garlic, rosemary, and oil from the pans. Transfer any remaining oil to a gravy boat and pass separately. If desired, serve with hot sauce.

Serves 8

Acknowledgments

I owe my editor, Rebecca Saletan, an enormous debt of gratitude. She never broke a promise, missed a deadline, or cared less than I did about even a comma. If my mother could have known her, she would have approved.

I would like to also thank my agent, Eric Simonoff, for offering tea, sympathy, and smarts, and making me feel secure in the knowledge that at least one of us is a grown-up.

Caroline Harrison, who has taken care of my mother since April 2006, is a blessing to our entire family. She is a warm, caring person who could not treat my mom any better if she were her own.

Evelyn Witchel, my aunt Kiki, has helped me run my mom's household from afar for seven years now. She is sharp, meticulous, and exacting in her tasks, patient and understanding in her manner, and fun to talk to late at night. She has helped me keep my sanity.

For the high level of care they have given my mom, I am indebted to Dr. Martin Goldstein, Dr. Jesse Weinberger, Dr. Robert

Novick, and Roberta Epstein. I owe special thanks to Dr. Jerome Groopman, who is the patron saint of *tsuris*, and offers excellent advice, always.

At the *Times*, I am grateful to my fine "Feed Me" editors, Sam Sifton and Pete Wells; at the magazine, I am indebted to my editors, Sheila Glaser and Rob Hoerburger, for their consistently excellent work.

I am also grateful to Sally Engel, Barbara Denner, Nicole Nicholas, Cynthia LaBorde, Susan Burden, Denise Landis, and Marcia Babbitt for all sorts of help, all of it appreciated.

A special thanks to my dear friend Philip Nicholas for creating Chicken with Rosemary and Garlic and for being my family these last four decades. Also to John Montorio, my friend and longtime editor, for always having my back.

I reserve my deepest thanks for my stepsons, Nathaniel and Simon Rich, and my husband, Frank Rich. Nat's steady patience and quiet kindness are always a boon; Simon's enthusiasm and encouragement jolted me into writing this book. Frank is, quite simply, the best person there is. To wake up with him each morning remains the greatest gift of my life.